Jeff Lantos

Why Longfellow Lied

The Truth About Paul Revere's Midnight Ride

Charlesbridge

For LeeAn

At the time of publication, all URLs printed in this book were accurate and active. Charlesbridge and the author are not responsible for the content or accessibility of any website.

Published by Charlesbridge
9 Galen Street
Watertown, MA 02472
(617) 926-0329
www.charlesbridge.com

Library of Congress Cataloging-in-Publication Data
Names: Lantos, Jeff, author.
Title: Why Longfellow lied: the truth about Paul Revere's midnight ride / Jeff Lantos.
Description: Watertown, MA: Charlesbridge, [2021] | Includes bibliographical references.
Identifiers: LCCN 2018052499 (print) | LCCN 2018056788 (ebook) | ISBN 9781632897848 (ebook) | ISBN 9781580899338 (reinforced for library use)
Subjects: LCSH: Longfellow, Henry Wadsworth, 1807–1882. Paul Revere's ride—Juvenile literature. | Longfellow, Henry Wadsworth, 1807–1882—Criticism and interpretation—Juvenile literature. | Revere, Paul, 1735–1818—Juvenile literature. Massachusetts—History—Revolution, 1775–1783—Juvenile literature.
Classification: LCC PS2271.P33 (ebook) | LCC PS2271.P33 L36 2019 (print) | DDC 811/.3—dc23
LC record available at https://lccn.loc.gov/2018052499

Printed in China
(hc) 10 9 8 7 6 5 4 3 2 1

Display type set in Hallowen by cruzine and Bold Riley by Simon Stratford
Text type set in Arethusa Pro by Aviation Partners
Printed by 1010 Printing International Limited in Huizhou, Guangdong, China
Production supervision by Jennifer Most Delaney
Designed by Diane M. Earley

Title page: Paul Revere statue on Paul Revere Mall in the North End of Boston, with the Old North Church steeple in the background.

Contents

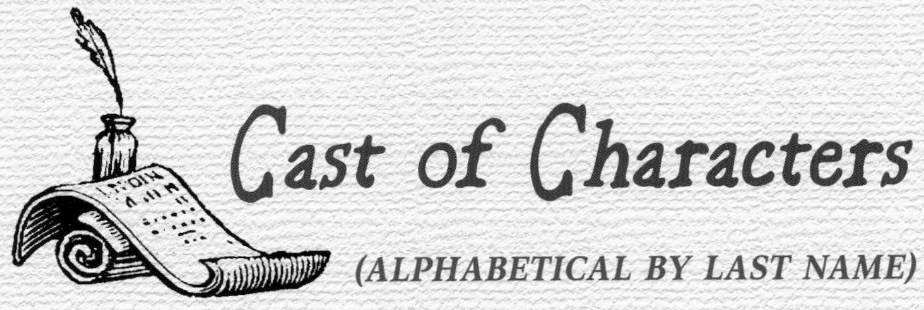

Cast of Characters

(ALPHABETICAL BY LAST NAME)

Lieutenant Jesse Adair—British officer

John Adams—Boston lawyer and Samuel Adams's younger cousin

Samuel Adams—patriot leader wanted by the British

Nathan Appleton—Longfellow's wealthy father-in-law

Nathaniel Baker—Lincoln minuteman

Thomas Barnard—Revere's operative

Amos Barrett—Concord minuteman

James Barrett—commander of the Concord militia

Nathan Barrett III—James Barrett's grandson

Jeremy Belknap—corresponding secretary of the Massachusetts Historical Society who pestered Revere for an account of his ride

Joshua Bentley—Revere's boatman

Luther Blanchard—Acton fifer

Thaddeus Blood—Concord minuteman

Solomon Bowman—minuteman officer in Menotomy (later Arlington)

Thaddeus Bowman—Lexington scout

Reverend Edward Brooks—Medford patriot

Joshua Brooks—Lincoln minuteman

Reuben Brown—Concord saddler and alarm rider

J. T. Buckingham—a magazine publisher who published Revere's account of his ride

John Buttrick—patriot commander at the North Bridge fight

Robert Byrd—West Virginia senator from 1959–2010

Reverend Jonas Clarke—Lexington clergyman

Cuff—John Hancock's slave

Cyrus Dallin—sculptor

Ezekiel Davis—Acton minuteman

Isaac Davis—captain of Acton minutemen

William Dawes—patriot alarm rider

William Diamond—Lexington drummer

Reverend William Emerson—Concord patriot and religious leader

William Eustis—Dr. Warren's apprentice

Edmund Foster—college student who joined Reading minutemen

Margaret Kemble Gage—American-born wife of General Gage

General Thomas Gage—commander of British forces in Boston

King George III—English king at the time of the Revolutionary War

Isaac Hall—captain of the Medford minutemen

John Hancock—patriot leader wanted by the British

Lydia Hancock—John Hancock's elderly aunt

Jonathan Harrington—Lexington fifer

Samuel Hartwell—sergeant of the Lincoln minutemen

Jonathan Hastings—Harvard administrator who offered his house for the patriot cause

Dr. Martin Herrick—impromptu patriot alarm rider

Abner Hosmer—Acton minuteman killed at North Bridge

Joseph Hosmer—Concord patriot who called for an attack on the British

Mrs. Abigail Jones—widow of Woburn minister Thomas Jones

Elisha Jones—Concord patriot

Edward M. (Ted) Kennedy—Massachusetts senator from 1962–2009

Captain Walter Laurie—British officer at the North Bridge

Abraham Lincoln—sixteenth president of the United States; served during the Civil War

Ensign Jeremy Lister—British officer wounded at Elm Brook

Abel Locke—a shoemaker in Menotomy (later Arlington)

Benjamin Locke—minuteman captain in Menotomy (later Arlington)

Alice Longfellow—Longfellow's oldest daughter

Ernest Longfellow—Longfellow's second son

Fanny Appleton Longfellow—Longfellow's wife

Henry Wadsworth Longfellow—world-famous poet

John Lowell—John Hancock's secretary

Major Edward Mitchell—British officer who interrogated Revere

William Munroe—militia officer in Lexington

Robert Newman—Revere's lantern man

John Parker—captain of Lexington militia

Captain Lawrence Parsons—British officer who searched James Barrett's farm

General Hugh Percy—British officer who reinforced Colonel Smith

Major John Pitcairn—British officer who gave orders on Lexington Common

Dr. Abel Prescott Jr.—Samuel's brother and impromptu alarm rider

Dr. Samuel Prescott—Concord man who teamed up with Revere and Dawes

John Pulling—Revere's lantern man

Dorothy "Dolly" Quincy—John Hancock's fiancée (later wife)

Paul Revere—patriot alarm rider

Rachel Revere—Revere's wife

Thomas Richardson—Revere's boatman

Isaac Royall—Medford loyalist

Elijah Sanderson—Lexington patriot captured by the British

Colonel Francis Smith—commander of the British march to Concord

Solomon Smith—Acton minuteman

Ebenezer Stedman—Cambridge militia captain

Sukey—a slave woman living in Lincoln

Charles Sumner—Massachusetts senator from 1851–1874; Longfellow's best friend

Lieutenant William Sutherland—British officer wounded at North Bridge

Elizabeth Taylor—Nathaniel Baker's girlfriend (later wife)

Thomas Thorp—Acton minuteman

John Trull—captain of the Tewksbury minutemen

Francis Underwood—editor of the *Atlantic Monthly*

John Vassall—Loyalist businessman

Winifred and **Marcellus Wagner**—young Longfellow correspondent and her brother

Dr. Joseph Warren—patriot spymaster and Revere's boss

George Washington—Revolutionary War general (later the first president of the United States)

Amos Wood—Concord patriot

Amos Wyman—patriot

Art is not truth.
Art is a lie that enables us to recognize truth.

—Pablo Picasso

Nor let the Historian blame the Poet here,
If he perchance misdate the day or year,
And group events together, by his art,
That in the Chronicles lie far apart;
For as the double stars, though sundered far,
Seem to the naked eye a single star,
So facts of history, at a distance seen,
Into one common point of light convene.

—Henry Wadsworth Longfellow,
Christus: A Mystery

Introduction

You'll Thank Me

In the twenty-five years between 1856 and 1881, if you wanted to send a letter to poet Henry Wadsworth Longfellow, all you had to do was put his name on the envelope, and the letter carrier would deliver it to his home at 105 Brattle Street in Cambridge, Massachusetts. Longfellow said the pile of fan mail on his desk looked like a "dirty snowdrift."

The Houghton Library at Harvard University has seventy-three boxes of Longfellow's mail and the names of more than 6,200 people who wrote to him. One of them was eight-year-old Winifred Wagner of Oil City, Pennsylvania. On February 28, 1881, she wrote, "In the A class Primary room . . . we celebrated your birthday today as yesterday was the Sabbath. . . . I spoke Paul Revere's ride. We had thirty visitors. . . . While I was committing my piece [to memory], my little brother, Marcellus (. . . he is three years old), learned nearly all of Paul Revere's ride. I have only to tell him now and then a word."

So to you, my dear readers, I say, Why not make like Winifred and little Marcellus and "speak" "Paul Revere's Ride"? You'll sharpen your mind, you'll impress your teacher, and you'll help perpetuate our cultural heritage. Too much work, you say? Then team up with a few friends or classmates, and each of you take a stanza or two. Still wavering? Okay, how about this: together we'll uncover what really happened on the eighteenth and nineteenth of April 1775. And then I bet you might want to memorize and recite the poem. It'll be win-win. In the end, you'll thank me.

Henry Wadsworth Longfellow in 1860, around the time he wrote "Paul Revere's Ride."

The Poem

"Paul Revere's Ride"

Paul Revere's Ride

by Henry Wadsworth Longfellow

Listen, my children, and you shall hear
Of the midnight ride of Paul Revere,
On the eighteenth of April, in Seventy-five;
Hardly a man is now alive
Who remembers that famous day and year.

He said to his friend, "If the British march
By land or sea from the town to-night,
Hang a lantern aloft in the belfry arch
Of the North Church tower as a signal light,—
One, if by land, and two, if by sea;
And I on the opposite shore will be,
Ready to ride and spread the alarm
Through every Middlesex village and farm,
For the country-folk to be up and to arm."

Then he said, "Good night!" and with muffled oar
Silently rowed to the Charlestown shore,
Just as the moon rose over the bay,
Where swinging wide at her moorings lay
The Somerset, British man-of-war;
A phantom ship, with each mast and spar
Across the moon like a prison bar,
And a huge black hulk, that was magnified
By its own reflection in the tide.

Meanwhile, his friend, through alley and street
Wanders and watches with eager ears,
Till in the silence around him he hears
The muster of men at the barrack door,
The sound of arms, and the tramp of feet,
And the measured tread of the grenadiers,
Marching down to their boats on the shore.

Then he climbed to the tower of the church,
Up the wooden stairs, with stealthy tread,
To the belfry-chamber overhead,
And startled the pigeons from their perch
On the sombre rafters, that round him made
Masses and moving shapes of shade,—
Up the trembling ladder, steep and tall,
To the highest window in the wall,

Where he paused to listen and look down
A moment on the roofs of the town,
And the moonlight flowing over all.

Beneath, in the churchyard, lay the dead,
In their night-encampment on the hill,
Wrapped in silence so deep and still
That he could hear, like a sentinel's tread,
The watchful night-wind, as it went
Creeping along from tent to tent,
And seeming to whisper, "All is well!"
A moment only he feels the spell
Of the place and the hour, and the secret dread
Of the lonely belfry and the dead;
For suddenly all his thoughts are bent
On a shadowy something far away,
Where the river widens to meet the bay,—
A line of black that bends and floats
On the rising tide, like a bridge of boats.

Meanwhile, impatient to mount and ride,
Booted and spurred, with a heavy stride
On the opposite shore walked Paul Revere.
Now he patted his horse's side,
Now gazed at the landscape far and near,
Then, impetuous, stamped the earth,

And turned and tightened his saddle-girth;
But mostly he watched with eager search
The belfry-tower of the Old North Church,
As it rose above the graves on the hill,
Lonely and spectral and sombre and still.
And lo! as he looks, on the belfry's height
A glimmer, and then a gleam of light!
He springs to the saddle, the bridle he turns,
But lingers and gazes, till full on his sight
A second lamp in the belfry burns!

A hurry of hoofs in a village street,
A shape in the moonlight, a bulk in the dark,
And beneath, from the pebbles, in passing, a spark
Struck out by a steed flying fearless and fleet;
That was all! And yet, through the gloom and the light,
The fate of a nation was riding that night;
And the spark struck out by that steed, in his flight,
Kindled the land into flame with its heat.
He has left the village and mounted the steep,
And beneath him, tranquil and broad and deep,
Is the Mystic, meeting the ocean tides;
And under the alders, that skirt its edge,
Now soft on the sand, now loud on the ledge,
Is heard the tramp of his steed as he rides.

Paul Revere calling out to warn people that "the Regulars are coming out tonight!" Artist unknown.

It was twelve by the village clock
When he crossed the bridge into Medford town.
He heard the crowing of the cock,
And the barking of the farmer's dog,
And felt the damp of the river fog,
That rises after the sun goes down.

It was one by the village clock,
When he galloped into Lexington.
He saw the gilded weathercock
Swim in the moonlight as he passed,
And the meeting-house windows, blank and bare,
Gaze at him with a spectral glare,
As if they already stood aghast
At the bloody work they would look upon.

It was two by the village clock,
When he came to the bridge in Concord town.
He heard the bleating of the flock,
And the twitter of birds among the trees,
And felt the breath of the morning breeze
Blowing over the meadows brown.
And one was safe and asleep in his bed
Who at the bridge would be first to fall,
Who that day would be lying dead,
Pierced by a British musket-ball.

You know the rest. In the books you have read,
How the British Regulars fired and fled,—
How the farmers gave them ball for ball,
From behind each fence and farm-yard wall,
Chasing the red-coats down the lane,
Then crossing the fields to emerge again
Under the trees at the turn of the road,
And only pausing to fire and load.

So through the night rode Paul Revere;
And so through the night went his cry of alarm
To every Middlesex village and farm,—
A cry of defiance and not of fear,
A voice in the darkness, a knock at the door,
And a word that shall echo forevermore!
For, borne on the night-wind of the Past,
Through all our history, to the last,
In the hour of darkness and peril and need,
The people will waken and listen to hear
The hurrying hoof-beats of that steed,
And the midnight message of Paul Revere.

The poem first appeared in print on December 18, 1860, in the *Boston Evening Transcript* and was reproduced in the January 1861 issue of the *Atlantic Monthly.* It was first published in book form in *Tales of a Wayside Inn* (Ticknor and Fields: Boston, 1863, pp. 18–25); that version appears here.

A photograph of the 1768 John Singleton Copley oil painting of Paul Revere, silversmith. The painting is in the Museum of Fine Arts, Boston, Massachusetts.

Prologue

Why So Quiet?

In the days, weeks, and months following Paul Revere's daring midnight ride, no one, it seemed, wanted to cheer about it. Heck, no one even wanted to *acknowledge* it. John Adams, who usually commented on everything, wrote nothing. Neither did his cousin, Samuel Adams, one of the two patriot leaders for whom Revere had risked life and limb. The other patriot leader Revere warned was John Hancock, and guess what he had to say about Revere's ride? Zilch. Ditto for the New England newspapers.

When Revere submitted a sworn deposition to the Massachusetts Provincial Congress about his ride and the subsequent Battle of Lexington, they sent it back to him. Then they went ahead and published twelve less informative (and suspiciously similar) accounts.

In the early histories of the American Revolution (those appearing between 1788 and 1805), authors who wrote about April 18 and 19, 1775, refer only to "messengers" and "travelers" and "intelligence . . . being transmitted to the country militia." Historian Edmund Morgan writes that "the part played by Paul Revere was scanted, and his name was not even mentioned."

And when Revere died in 1818 at age eighty-three, the Boston papers lauded him for his sound opinions, public service, and patriotic zeal, but not a single obituary highlighted his midnight ride.

Why this historical hush? Why not give Revere his due? Here's why: He didn't fit into the mythical narrative that Boston's patriot leaders had crafted and wished to perpetuate. That narrative insisted that American colonists were the innocent and law-abiding victims of barbarous British aggression. A midnight rider carrying out a curfew-defying secret mission could hardly be called innocent or law-abiding. So Revere was cut from the narrative. Even long after the war, Boston's aging patriots (or Whigs, as they were called) felt it best to keep secret missions secret.

But let's face it: Paul Revere's ride was too good a story to suppress completely, and you can be sure that in and around Revere's neighborhood in the North End of Boston, moms and dads regaled their kids with tales of Revere's derring-do. Long afterward, one of those neighborhood kids recalled that the story of the flashing lanterns and the midnight ride was "common talk at [his] father's, where [Whig leaders] often met, although . . . they were careful of [mentioning] names, having some fear of liability." Another child remembered, "We needed no fairy tales in our youth. The real experiences of our own people were more fascinating than all the novels ever written."

Every April 18 and 19, it's easy to imagine that old codgers in the countryside reminisced about the galloping hoofbeats and the cry of alarm. Even so, it seemed that Paul Revere was destined to go down in history as no more than a local folk hero.

But then, in 1832, nearly sixty years after Revere's ride, everything changed. That's when a Boston-based

Bye-bye, Bordeaux; Hello, Boston

In 1685, French king Louis XIV ruled that only Catholics could live in France. Paul Revere's paternal ancestors were Huguenots (Protestants). So they packed up and fled. Had King Louis been a little nicer or a little more tolerant, Paul Revere might have grown up in Bordeaux, stomping on grapes, eating smelly cheese, and answering to the name of Apollos Rivoire.

magazine publisher named J. T. Buckingham burrowed into the archives of the Massachusetts Historical Society and emerged with a letter that Revere had written to Jeremy Belknap, the corresponding secretary of the society. Belknap had been after Revere to tell his story, and in January 1798, "having a little leisure," Revere finally sat down and wrote "some facts and anecdotes prior to the Battle of Lexington." Buckingham published the letter in the October 1832 issue of his *New-England Magazine*, and he assured his readers that Revere's account contained "incident enough to supply a novelist with the basis" of a heroic adventure.

To be clear, the surfacing of that old letter, by itself, would not have been enough to rocket Revere to everlasting fame. But it just so happened that in that same issue of Buckingham's magazine, there was an English translation of an ancient French tale about a really lousy king. The translation was done by a twenty-five-year-old professor of modern languages at Bowdoin College in Brunswick, Maine. His name was Henry Wadsworth Longfellow, and while riffling through his copy of *New-England Magazine*, he came across Revere's letter. Like Buckingham, he was riveted, and he added Revere's midnight ride to his list of topics to write about someday.

Before that day came, a lot would change in Longfellow's life. He would

Right Address, Wrong Writer

A letter Longfellow received from Germany was addressed: "To the right honorable Mr. Henry Wadsworth Longfellow, celebrated poet, in America, near Boston." At the time, there was one other American who often received mail with only his name on the envelope. That was P. T. Barnum, the great showman and founder of the Barnum & Bailey Circus.

Many Longfellow fans did more than write. Some traveled to Cambridge, Massachusetts, and showed up at the poet's house. One such fan was so awestruck when Longfellow opened the door, he forgot which famous writer he was looking for. The man asked, "Does William Shakespeare live nearby?" Longfellow said, "I know of no such person in the neighborhood."

accept a job at Harvard; move to Cambridge; marry his dream girl, Fanny Appleton; and have six children (five of whom survived childhood). He'd also deliver hundreds of lectures about renowned writers like Dante, Molière, Goethe, and Cervantes; he'd travel twice to Europe to learn, or brush up on, his German, French, Spanish, Italian, Portuguese, Dutch, Danish, Swedish, Finnish, and Icelandic; and he'd publish scads of popular poems, including "The Village Blacksmith," "The Wreck of the Hesperus," and "The Courtship of Miles Standish." That last one was published on October 16, 1858, and that day, five thousand copies were sold in Boston and twice that many in London.

A year and a half later, on an early spring day in 1860, while Abraham Lincoln campaigned for president and lawmakers in Washington, DC, debated about the issue of slavery, Longfellow decided it was finally time to get poetic with that Revere narrative he'd read nearly three decades earlier. Never one to stint on research, the poet took a hike through the North End of Boston. After passing Revere's two-story house on North Square, he rambled around Hull Street and Copp's Hill Burying Ground. At the old North Church, Longfellow climbed the stairs to the highest window. In his journal he noted, "From this tower were hung the lanterns as a signal that . . . the British troops had left Boston for Concord." He also noted the "innumerable pigeons."

The next day, April 6, 1860, Longfellow began writing his most famous poem. It begins like this:

Listen, my children, and you shall hear
Of the midnight ride of Paul Revere,

There is no finer opening sentence. This is a master storyteller inviting little ones to gather round and get ready for an enthralling bedtime story. In how many houses throughout the world did moms or dads read those words before a blazing fire? Henry Longfellow created family entertainment seventy years before Walt Disney.

Longfellow wrote this indelible opening couplet in the ground-floor study of his Brattle Street home in Cambridge. A fine example of symmetry and simplicity, the house was built in 1759 by John Vassall, a sugar baron who later remained loyal to England's King George III. Bad decision. Finding himself on the wrong side of the conflict, Vassall (along with other wealthy loyalists) fled Boston in 1774. Guess who moved into Vassall's house the next year? George Washington! Yes, the home became General Washington's headquarters during the first nine months of the American Revolution. Sixty-eight years later, in 1843 (with major financial help from his father-in-law, Nathan Appleton), Longfellow bought the place. Showing his study to a visitor, Longfellow said, "Where my writing desk now stands, there stood [Washington's] table." Washington's orders to his troops and his letters to Congress, Longfellow noted, were drafted "perhaps in this very room, – certainly in this very house."

In one corner of the study stood a grandfather clock. Alice Longfellow, the poet's oldest daughter, recalled that "its measured tick-tock made the most delicious accompaniment to a story book read by the open soft-coal

The Lady and the Tramp

Later in life, Longfellow enjoyed taking long walks and was a familiar figure on the streets of Cambridge, Massachusetts. One day near the Harvard Botanic Garden, he had a friendly conversation with two children. They told their mother about the white-haired man, and she warned them to keep out of his way.

"He might be a tramp," she said. "And tramps are dangerous."

Not long afterward, the children met the poet again, and the boy asked him, "Are you a tramp? Mother thinks you're a tramp, and she wants to know what your name is."

Longfellow said, "I may call myself a tramp. I tramp a great deal; but you may tell your mother that my name is Henry W. Longfellow." He later visited the mother and congratulated her "on having such fine children."

fire on a stormy day." In front of the south-facing windows, the poet placed a ten-foot-high lemon tree that he said "kept up a make-believe summer all winter long." Through the tree branches, Longfellow could gaze at the Charles River, which was "stealing onward," he wrote, "like the stream of life."

Books were everywhere in the house, and Alice remembered that her father was "constantly arranging and rearranging them and handling them as he would a child." A visitor noted that "even closets supposed to be devoted to pails and dust-cloths had three shelves for books and one for pails." If you knew where to look, you could find one drawer in one bookcase that remained book-free. This drawer, said Alice, was "dedicated to small cakes of chocolate for cases of extreme need, and rarely did the supply fail."

The house where Longfellow lived in Cambridge, Massachusetts, is now the Longfellow House–Washington's Headquarters National Historical Site and is open to visitors.

A typical morning found Longfellow rising early and taking a long stroll with his beloved Scottish terrier Trap. Returning home, he enjoyed a breakfast of oatmeal and milk before disappearing into his study, where "he wrote standing at a desk by one of the front windows." When he wearied of standing, he moved either to a round table in the center of the room or to a cushy armchair near the fireplace. While in this armchair, Longfellow often dozed off and started snoring. This disturbed Trap, who was dozing near the heating vent. To quiet his master, Trap walked over and pawed Longfellow's knee until the poet awoke. "There was something so human about this," wrote Longfellow's son Ernest, "that my father never resented it."

Before setting pencil to paper, the poet always donned a dress coat and tie. "He was fond of elegance," Alice remembered, and never wore anything "that was at all untidy or unattractive." If roses were in bloom, he'd stick one on his lapel. He did this, he said, out of respect for his readers.

Standing at his desk, his back "perfectly erect," his hand steady, a few streaks of gray among his wavy brown hair, the smartly dressed Longfellow followed his memorable first lines with the narrative nitty-gritty: a furtive friend, muffled oars, the rising moon, a fearsome British warship, the marching soldiers, the climb to the belfry, town-to-town sprints, ticking clocks, and the bloody shootout on the Battle Road. All that, plus some nifty rhymes and a soul-stirring final stanza. Wow! No wonder the "snowdrift" of fan mail. No wonder men stood and doffed their caps when the poet climbed aboard a Cambridge horse car. And no wonder the *New York Ledger* offered Longfellow one thousand dollars for ten poems of any length.

On the eighteenth of April, in Seventy-five;
Hardly a man is now alive
Who remembers that famous day and year.

Few poems include an exact day, month, and year. But Longfellow wanted his readers to remember that famous April day and year when two very different fighting forces were set in motion: one well dressed, well equipped, and well drilled; the other unpolished, untested, and unpredictable. The following morning (April 19, 1775) on the common in Lexington, and a few hours later at the North Bridge in Concord, these forces collided. When that happened—when that first Massachusetts musket ball ripped through a British redcoat—it made a tiny tear in the fabric of the mighty British Empire, a tear that would eventually lead to a great unraveling and the birth of a new nation: the United States of America.

The Battle of Lexington, April 1775 *was created by artist Amos Doolittle and it was once printed as part of a Connecticut Historical Society calendar.*

Wait! Don't get all swoony and misty-eyed. Don't start waving a flag and belting out "The Star-Spangled Banner," at least not until we've discussed one problem with the poem. Once you get past the catchy opening and the narrative razzle-dazzle, Mr. Longfellow's masterpiece doesn't adhere to the facts. Or, as historian David Hackett Fischer puts it, the poem is "grossly, systematically and deliberately inaccurate."

Yes. Longfellow lied.

After the poem was published, some of Longfellow's contemporaries expressed their dismay. Cambridge lawyer Henry Holland noted, "The facts about Revere . . . are . . . very different from Longfellow's vivid sketch." Lexington town historian Charles Hudson wrote that he was well acquainted with poetic license, but he thought such license should be "confined to . . . regions of the imagination, and should not extend to historic facts." He added, "When poets pervert plain matters of history, . . . they should be restrained."

Well, restraining Longfellow is no longer an option, since he died in 1882. But that doesn't mean we should stay silent and do nothing. Silence and inaction have left generations of readers stranded in a no-man's-land between historical facts and poetic whimsy. It's time to stand with our stranded brothers and sisters and say, "Enough! Too many have been misled for too long!"

Here's the action plan: We'll go through the poem, stanza by stanza, and compare Longfellow's version of events to the written accounts of the men and women who were there in Boston, in Lexington, in Concord, and along the Battle Road. We'll pinpoint exactly where Longfellow veered from the historical record. And finally, we'll ponder (and answer!) a big question: Why did he do it? Why did Longfellow lie?

Major General Joseph Warren, later killed at the Battle of Bunker Hill on June 17, 1775.

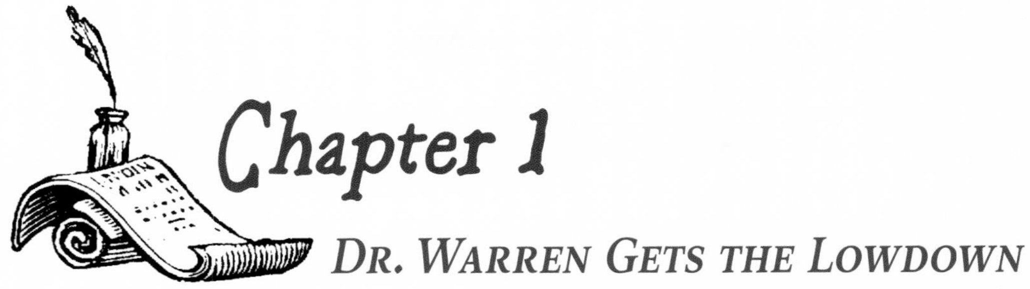

Chapter 1

Dr. Warren Gets the Lowdown

He said to his friend, "If the British march
By land or sea from the town to-night,
Hang a lantern aloft in the belfry arch
Of the North Church tower as a signal light,—
One, if by land, and two, if by sea;
And I on the opposite shore will be,
Ready to ride and spread the alarm
Through every Middlesex village and farm,
For the country-folk to be up and to arm."

There's a lot to straighten out in this section of the poem. Let's start with this: Paul Revere would not have galloped anywhere if he hadn't been told to do so by his boss, the brilliant patriot spymaster Dr. Joseph Warren. Revere was the arrow; Warren was the bow.

By mid-April 1775, the thirty-three-year-old Warren was the only patriot leader left in Boston. Fearing arrest, John Hancock, Samuel Adams, and other big Whigs had fled to the countryside. Dr. Warren was worried about being arrested, but he refused to abandon the men, women, and children under his medical care. He did, however, pack two pistols when making house calls.

Give the patriots some credit here. Appointing a doctor as their spymaster was a shrewd idea. Anyone with a limp, a cough, a sniffle, or a bandage could walk into Warren's consulting room without arousing suspicion. Behind closed doors, Warren could get the lowdown not only from his patients but also from patriot spies pretending to be patients, and from healthy young women who made appointments so they could flirt with the handsome and recently widowed doctor.

In the early afternoon of April 18, Warren received a report that twenty mounted British soldiers—ten officers and ten sergeants—had ridden out of Boston on Orange Street, the one road that crossed Boston Neck.

Don't look for the Neck on a current map. It's long gone. In the nineteenth century, Boston's five hills were shorn, or leveled, and all that dirt was dumped into Boston Harbor and used to widen the city. But in 1775, before that expansion, the Neck was the only land bridge, or isthmus, that connected the narrow peninsula of Boston to the rest of Massachusetts. About a mile long and 120 feet wide, the Neck stretched from South Boston to Dorchester. It was home to ducks, egrets, herons, and highway robbers known to make their getaway in canoes and rowboats. In April that year, the Neck was also home to 340 British soldiers who worked the guardhouse, the blockhouse, and the town gate.

British soldiers (also known as regulars or redcoats) often marched or rode over the Neck. Since late March 1775, the British commander in chief, General Thomas Gage, had sent various regiments on four- to eight-mile hikes into the Massachusetts countryside.

A Whig Is Not a Wig

A Whig had nothing to do with fake hair. A Whig was a person who was no fan of kings or queens. Since the seventeenth century, "Whigs had consistently questioned the king's claim to unrestrained authority." After 1768, American colonists critical of British rule started calling themselves Whigs.

He wanted both to get his men in shape and "to familiarize the people of the country with the appearance of troops . . . without creating an alarm."

But hiking regulars and mounted officers usually left Boston in the early morning, not at two in the afternoon. Warren suspected the twenty mounted British soldiers were engaged in something other than a training exercise, but he needed more information. It didn't take long for him to get it. By late afternoon, Warren had received tips from a landlady, a gunsmith, a shop owner, a stableboy, and a distillery clerk. Based on what they had heard on the streets and seen in the harbor, all seemed to think a British invasion of the countryside was imminent, and the likely target was Concord, a town eighteen miles northwest of Boston. Why Concord? Because that's where the patriots had stockpiled tons of their military supplies. Several factors made Concord an ideal patriot depot. First, it was a crossroads town, so it was easy to cart supplies there from any direction. Second, with a robust population of fifteen hundred, there were plenty of houses, barns, haylofts, and wagon sheds in which to conceal the military "stores," as they were called. Third, the town was home to only a few loyalists. Fourth, Concord was a good six-hour march from Boston, and because it was inland, it wasn't reachable by British warships or transport boats.

A photograph of an engraving of General Gage, made circa 1899 by William Sartain.

On the British side, General Gage was eager to repeat an earlier success. Some eight months before, on September 1, 1774, he'd sent 260 regulars on a secret, early-morning

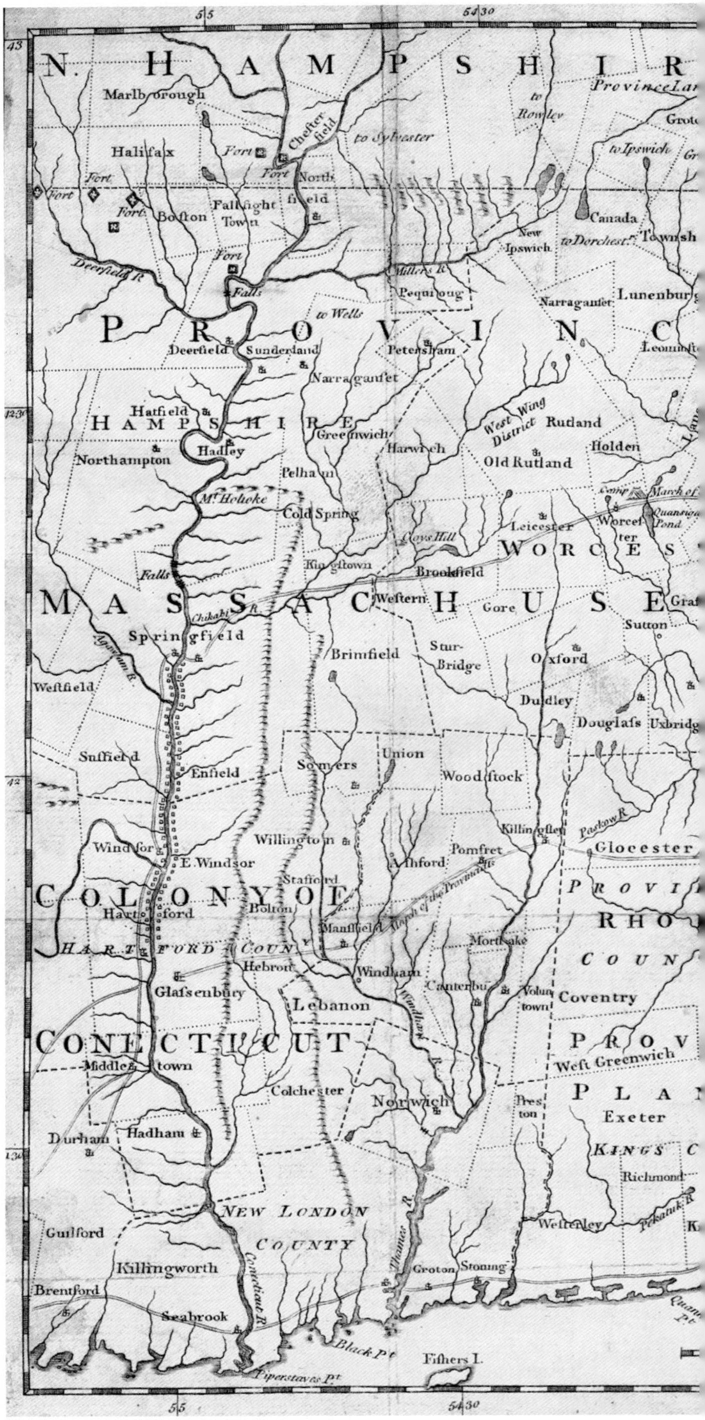

A 1775 map of southern New England printed in Universal Magazine. *Concord is circled in red. Lexington is nearby and Boston is farther to the east.*

mission up the Mystic River to Cambridge. Disembarking from their transport boats, the regulars hiked up Quarry Hill, on top of which sat a windowless, locked-up, stone tower called the Provincial Powder House. The loyalist sheriff met the regulars and handed over the keys to the powder house. Before the patriots woke up, the largest supply of gunpowder in New England had been removed, carried to the river, and shipped to the British camp in Boston.

After that flawless operation, Gage must have thought, "Why not go after more rebel military supplies?" There was only one problem. He didn't know where they were. So he sent two British spies disguised as farmers into the countryside. When they discovered the gigantic cache in Concord, General Gage began planning another surprise mission. He knew that without those supplies in Concord, the patriots could not field an army. And without an army, their threats were just talk.

As afternoon shadows lengthened, Dr. Warren had to make a decision. Twice in the past ten days—on April 8 and again on April 16—he had heard similar chatter about a secret march. Both times, he had sent Paul Revere—his ever-ready alarm rider—racing off to warn Concord. Both times, Warren had been wrong. He didn't want to be wrong a third time.

Warren went outside. Hanover Street was quiet. He walked over to Union Street. No sign of troop movements. Still, there was something that made Warren uneasy. Those twenty British soldiers had not returned.

Sunny Side Up

In March 1775, some British officers devised a plan to assassinate Dr. Warren while he gave a speech honoring the fifth anniversary of the Boston Massacre. The plan called for a soldier to throw a raw egg at Warren while he spoke. In the riot that was sure to follow, sword-wielding soldiers would rush the stage and slash the doctor. But the plan fizzled when, on his way into the meeting house, the egg-bearing soldier fell and cracked both the egg and his knee.

Soldiers who ventured into the countryside were usually back in Boston before supper. Where were they? What were they up to?

Warren decided he had to take the risky step of sending a messenger deep into the most dangerous part of Boston: General Gage's compound on Marlborough Street. There, Warren had a super-secret spy, someone who knew the most closely guarded secrets of the British high command. A friend of Warren's later reported that this spy was a woman. Now here's a historical surmise that will raise your eyebrows: That woman may have been none other than Margaret Kemble Gage, the wife of the British commander. Whoa—how could that happen? Well, first of all, Mrs. Gage was born in New Jersey, not England. She met Thomas Gage in 1757 when she was eighteen. At the time, Gage was in New Brunswick, New Jersey, to recruit men to fight the French army in Canada and to court the well-known and well-bred Miss Kemble. Both recruiting and courtship were successful, and the couple married a year later. By all accounts, the marriage was a happy one, but by 1775 Mrs. Gage was distressed about the brewing conflict between the mother country and the thirteen colonies. To a friend, she later admitted "that her own emotions were well described" by Lady Blanch in William Shakespeare's play *King John*. In the play, Lady Blanch asks, "Which is the side that I must go withal? I am with both."

A photograph of the 1771 John Singleton Copley oil painting of Margaret Kemble Gage, wife of General Gage. The painting is in the Timken Museum of Art, San Diego, California.

A second reason to suspect that Mrs. Gage was Dr. Warren's spy is

because two high-ranking British officers reported that later on the night of April 18, General Gage "was betrayed" by "someone very near to him."

Having been in Boston for over seven months, Mrs. Gage certainly knew of Dr. Warren, and she may have sought him out for her medical needs. After all, he treated prominent Bostonians (including loyalists), and being a family doctor, it was likely he knew more about women's maladies than British army surgeons did. If warm feelings developed between the charismatic doctor and this forty-one-year-old mom, it would not have been surprising. If and when the two of them discussed politics, Warren would have quickly realized that Mrs. Gage's loyalties were divided. She told a friend (and could have told Warren) that she "hoped her husband would never be the instrument of sacrificing the lives of her countrymen."

As yet, no document has been found to prove without a doubt that Mrs. Gage was Dr. Warren's super-secret spy. Historians are split on the subject. Allen French writes that suspicions regarding Mrs. Gage's conduct "belong to romance rather than history." But Professor Fischer concludes that it is "highly probable" that Mrs. Gage was Warren's informer. Let's say that

Powder to the People

After the British raid on the Cambridge powder house, Revere and his fellow artisans (or mechanics, as they were called) decided the Boston patriots needed better intelligence.

"I was one of thirty," Revere wrote, "who formed ourselves into a committee for the purpose of watching the movements of the British soldiers."

The men went out in pairs and patrolled the streets day and night. By early December, they had picked up enough chatter from the British camp to conclude that General Gage was planning to send a force to Portsmouth, New Hampshire, to retrieve ninety-seven barrels of gunpowder from an old British fort.

On Dr. Warren's orders, Revere saddled up and raced sixty miles over icy roads to warn the patriots in Portsmouth. Four hundred of these patriots mustered, marched to the fort, scaled the walls, subdued the six British soldiers inside, and made off with all the gunpowder.

whoever the informant was, Warren was told that General Gage had indeed ordered hundreds of regulars to be ferried across the Charles River that night. And yes, their mission was to destroy the colonial military supplies in Concord. And those twenty British soldiers had not returned for supper because they were patrolling the roads and intersections west of Boston. Gage had ordered them to nab any patriot alarm riders carrying a warning to Concord.

Between Boston and Concord, directly on the British line of march, was the town of Lexington. It was there, in the home of Lexington's religious leader, Reverend Jonas Clarke, that John Hancock and Samuel Adams had taken refuge.

The thirty-eight-year-old Hancock had moved into the Clarke home on April 7. His entourage included his elderly aunt Lydia and his twenty-seven-year-old fiancée, Dorothy "Dolly" Quincy.

Being both a dapper dresser and one of the richest men in the thirteen colonies, Hancock did not travel light. Strapped onto the back of his custom-made yellow coach was a tower of trunks filled with lace-trimmed shirts, blue velvet breeches, gilt-edged jackets, white silk stockings, and silver-buckled shoes, all imported from London.

Fifty-two-year-old Samuel Adams had arrived at the Clarke house on April 10. He had no entourage and no imported clothes. In fact, other than the threadbare suit and stockings he was wearing, Adams owned few other outfits. His wardrobe, writes one historian, was one of the "slenderest . . . in Boston."

It wasn't just wealth and wardrobe that set these two men apart. They were an odd couple in just about every way. Hancock was "nearly six feet in stature and of thin person." Adams was shorter and pear shaped. Hancock preferred the company of his rich fellow merchants. Adams was firm friends with the shipwrights, the biscuit bakers, the rope and sailcloth makers, and those from "the humblest walks of life."

John Hancock, created by J. B. Longacre.

Hancock was a "graceful speaker, self-possessed, and dignified." Adams had "a quavering voice and a shaky hand." Hancock's multicourse meals were lubricated with the finest imported wines. Adams was "frugal and temperate in his habits." To make sure every dinner included fresh fowl, Hancock kept 150 live turkeys in his coach house. Adams kept no turkeys, and his barn was falling down.

Mismatched though they were, the two men made a great team. Hancock brought the money and the political power. Samuel Adams brought the street smarts and the "artful pen." Together they rallied a group of patriots that included everyone from high-heeled gentlemen to barefoot sailors.

But leaders of rebellions attract notoriety, and sure enough, on April 4, 1775, Hancock and Adams found their names atop a list recently received from London. King George III wanted both men arrested, put on trial, found guilty, and executed.

On the night of April 18, Warren's super-secret spy told him that Hancock and Adams were in danger. A British officer later summed it up this way: "Our business was to seize a quantity of military stores and the bodies of . . . Hancock and Adams."

From Longfellow, we get none of this backstory. Readers of the poem have no idea why General Gage was sending eight hundred regulars into the Massachusetts countryside. Nor would you know that around eight

o'clock that evening, Dr. Warren sent for a burly thirty-year-old Boston tanner named William Dawes. The doctor had treated Dawes, knew he was a patriot, and trusted him. When the tanner arrived, Warren asked if he'd be willing to undertake the risky assignment of carrying a written warning to Hancock and Adams in Lexington. Dawes said he was willing. Leaving Warren's, Dawes did not go home to grab his riding coat and give his wife a smooch. There was no time for that. General Gage had ordered a nine o'clock curfew, and Dawes knew he had to get to Orange Street and over Boston Neck before British soldiers closed the town gate.

Samuel Adams depicted in a book illustration created by an unknown artist.

Great dramatic possibilities here, right? Dawes hurrying toward the Neck . . . a tense interrogation by the British guards . . . the town gate starting to close. Would Dawes make it out? But this, too, is missing from the poem. Instead, Longfellow keeps us focused on Paul Revere and whisks us to the waterfront where Revere parts with a friend and climbs into a rowboat.

Paul Revere's house, 19 North Square in Boston's North End, is now a museum. Revere sold the house in 1800, and it served as a boarding house, tenement apartments, and shops during the century that followed. In 1905 a group formed the Paul Revere Memorial Association, and the house opened to the public on April 18, 1908.

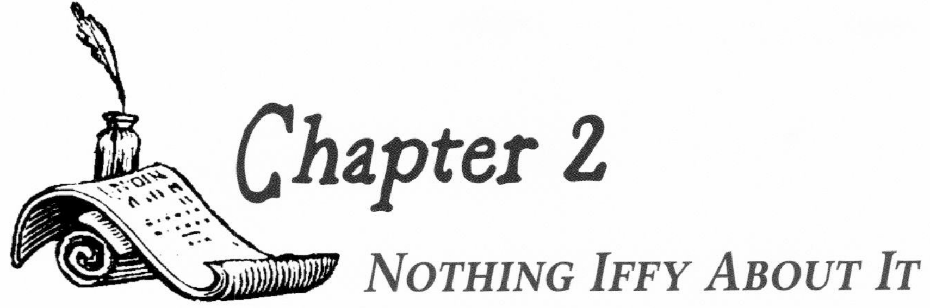

Chapter 2

Nothing Iffy About It

Then he said, "Good night!" and with muffled oar
Silently rowed to the Charlestown shore,

Okay, let's pause here, because we've got a timeline problem. Longfellow put Revere in the rowboat much too early. That's what happens when you cut Dr. Warren and William Dawes from your poem.

At this point in the actual story—say, around nine fifteen at night—Revere was at home, maybe reading a bedtime story to his six older children while his wife, Rachel, nursed four-month-old Joshua.

As for Dr. Warren, he was outside. He wanted to see for himself if the regulars were marching down to their boats on the shore. Again, Hanover Street was quiet. Ignoring General Gage's nine o'clock curfew, Warren and his apprentice, William Eustis, walked four blocks to Beacon Hill. From there they scanned the beach at the bottom of Boston Common. That's when they saw flickering pine torches on the shoreline. In the firelight of those torches, Warren and Eustis could see sailors, provision carts, and a scrum of transport boats. Into the torchlight walked the first regiment of regulars. Warren's super-secret agent was right. This was no drill. Warren told Eustis to go get Revere.

Warren and Revere had known each other for fourteen years. Despite the age difference (Revere was six years older), the class difference (gentleman versus artisan), and their different education levels (Harvard

versus grammar school), they had become friends. It was the British taxes—on molasses, sugar, paper, paint, glass, lead, and tea—that had turned both men into patriots. In December 1773, Warren had sent Revere on his first ride, down to New York City, where he delivered news about the destruction of tea, later known as the Boston Tea Party. Since then, Revere had logged close to three thousand miles delivering political messages far and near.

From Revere's two-story house on North Square, it was six blocks to Warren's apartment on Hanover Street. Revere arrived shortly before ten o'clock and later wrote that Warren "desired [him] to go to Lexington" to warn Adams and Hancock that "they were the objects" of a British manhunt. Revere was then to continue to Concord to report the threat to "the colony stores."

Warren also told Revere that he'd sent a duplicate message with William Dawes, but he had no idea if the tanner had made it across the Neck and into the countryside.

With Dawes attempting the southward land route, it's likely Warren urged Revere to head to the North End and try to leave Boston by rowboat. If he could make it across the Charles River, Revere knew that patriots in Charlestown would provide him with a horse. How did he know? Because two days earlier, after delivering the second false alarm to Lexington, Revere had "returned at night through

What's in a Name?

If you're wondering about the name Middlesex, it goes back to the fifth century, when southern England was invaded by Saxon tribes from northern Germany. Beginning in the year 477, the Saxons established minikingdoms all around London (or Londinium, as it was known then). The middle of the Saxon empire was known as Middle Saxony, later shortened to Middlesax, which morphed into Middlesex. Those west of Middlesex were West Saxons, and that area became known as Wessex. South was Sussex and east was Essex. There's no Norsex because the land in the north was settled by Danes, not Saxons.

Charlestown," where he had met local patriots who assured him they'd have a horse for him.

But what if no patriot could get across the Charles River or over Boston Neck? How could Bostonians get a message to the countryside? That's when the Charlestown patriots had hit on the idea of signal lanterns. Revere wrote, "I agreed with [the Charlestown] gentlemen, that if the British went out by water, we would show two lanterns in the North Church steeple; and if by land, one." (In fact, Revere didn't call them lanterns; he called them "lanthorns" because in 1775, the translucent lantern sides were made from "paper-thin slices of cow horn.") Revere had been put in charge of this lantern business, and the next day, April 17, he recruited three operatives. In all his writings Revere never identified who they were. He wouldn't even admit that there were three. "I left Dr. Warren's," he wrote, and "called upon a friend, and desired him to make the signals."

Photograph of one of the lanterns flashed from the church steeple the night of April 18, 1775. It is in the Concord Museum, Concord, Massachusetts.

Despite Revere's caution, people talk, and the names of the three operatives were "known in Boston soon after the event." One was John Pulling, and it was to his house, on the corner of Ann and Cross Streets, that Revere likely headed right after his meeting with Warren.

Pulling, age thirty-eight, was a longtime friend, but it was more than friendship that thrust him into this supporting role. There was also

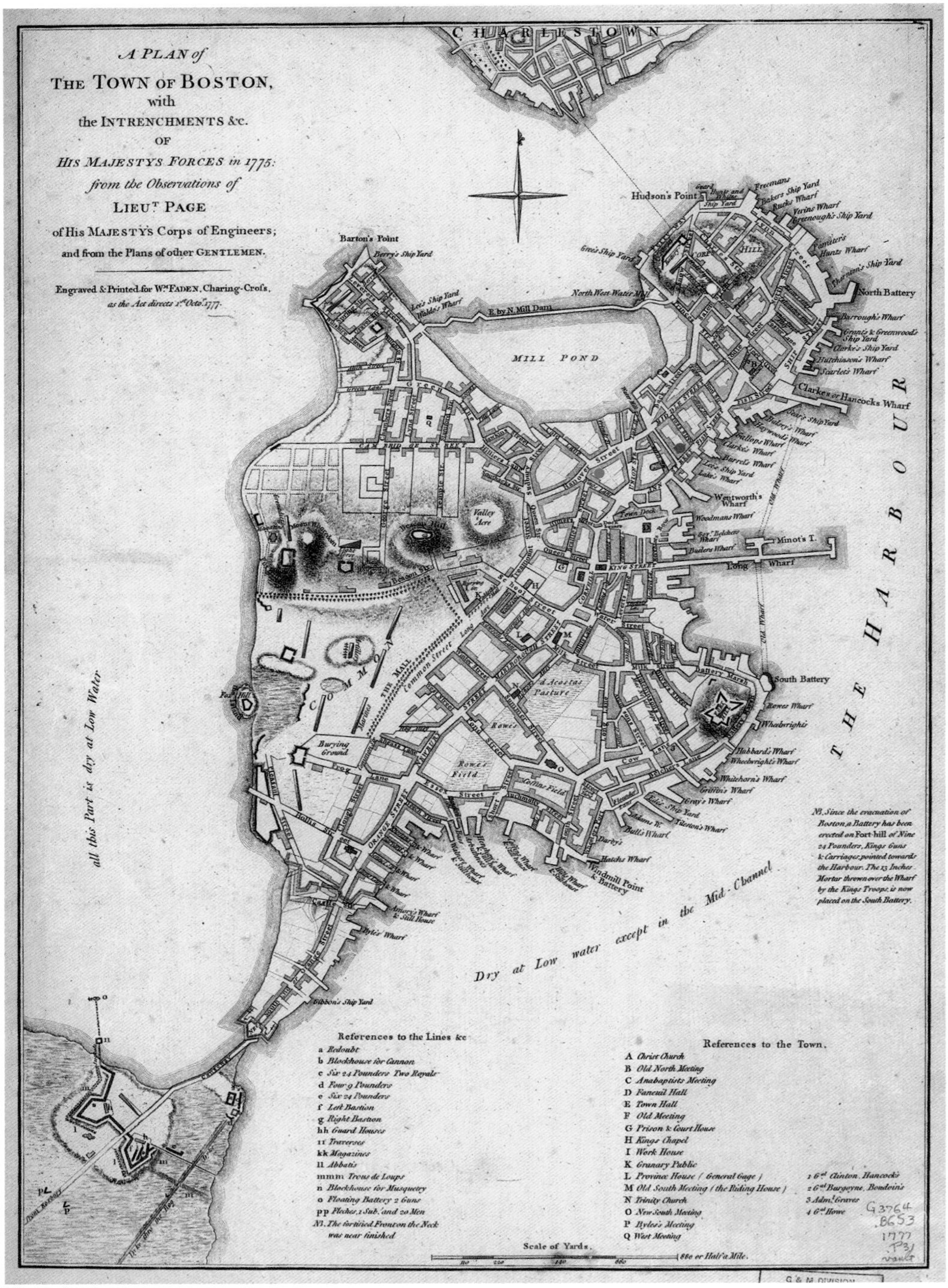

A PLAN of
THE TOWN OF BOSTON,
with
the INTRENCHMENTS &c.
OF
HIS MAJESTYS FORCES in 1775:
from the Observations of
LIEUT. PAGE
of His MAJESTY'S Corps of Engineers;
and from the Plans of other GENTLEMEN.

Engraved & Printed for Wm. FADEN, Charing-Cross, as the Act directs 1st. Octr. 1777.

Map of Boston, 1775. The yellow dot is the Newman house. The orange dot is the Revere house. The red dot is the Pulling house. The blue dot is the Warren house. The green dot is the Old North Church.

the fact that he was a vestryman at the North Church, meaning that any time of the day or night, Pulling could ask the groundskeeper to unlock the door to the church and let him into the sanctuary.

Revere knocked on Pulling's door. A bolt slid back, the door opened, and Pulling peeked out. What followed was likely a very short conversation, because all Revere had to say was, "Two lanterns."

In the poem, Longfellow had Revere say, "*If* the British march," but after his meeting with Warren, Revere *knew* the British were marching. Longfellow continued with the "ifs." He wrote, "One, if by land, and two, if by sea." Again, there was nothing iffy about it. Warren had told Revere the British were going by water, across the Charles River estuary.

Nor did Revere say to Pulling, "And I on the opposite shore will be," as Longfellow wrote. Revere had no idea if he would make it to the opposite shore. To do that, he'd have to get past the *Somerset*, the sixty-four-gun British warship anchored in the ferry way between Boston and Charlestown.

From Pulling's place, Revere likely hurried home to get his boots, spurs, and riding coat. Let's imagine a quick hug and kiss for wife Rachel, and then Revere was out the door, his boots crunching on the oyster shells that covered North Square.

Okay, *now* we're ready for the white-knuckle rowboat ride.

Warning: Gory Details Ahead

If the British had managed to arrest Hancock and Adams, they would have charged the two men with treason. In those days, the penalty for treason was terrifying. It was spelled out by a judge who read the following to some treasonous Irish rebels: "You are to be drawn on hurdles to the place of execution, where you are to be hanged by the neck, but not until you are dead; for, while you are still living your bodies are to be taken down, your bowels torn out and burned before your faces, your heads then cut off, and your bodies divided each into four quarters, and your heads and quarters to be then at the king's disposal; and may the Almighty God have mercy on your souls."

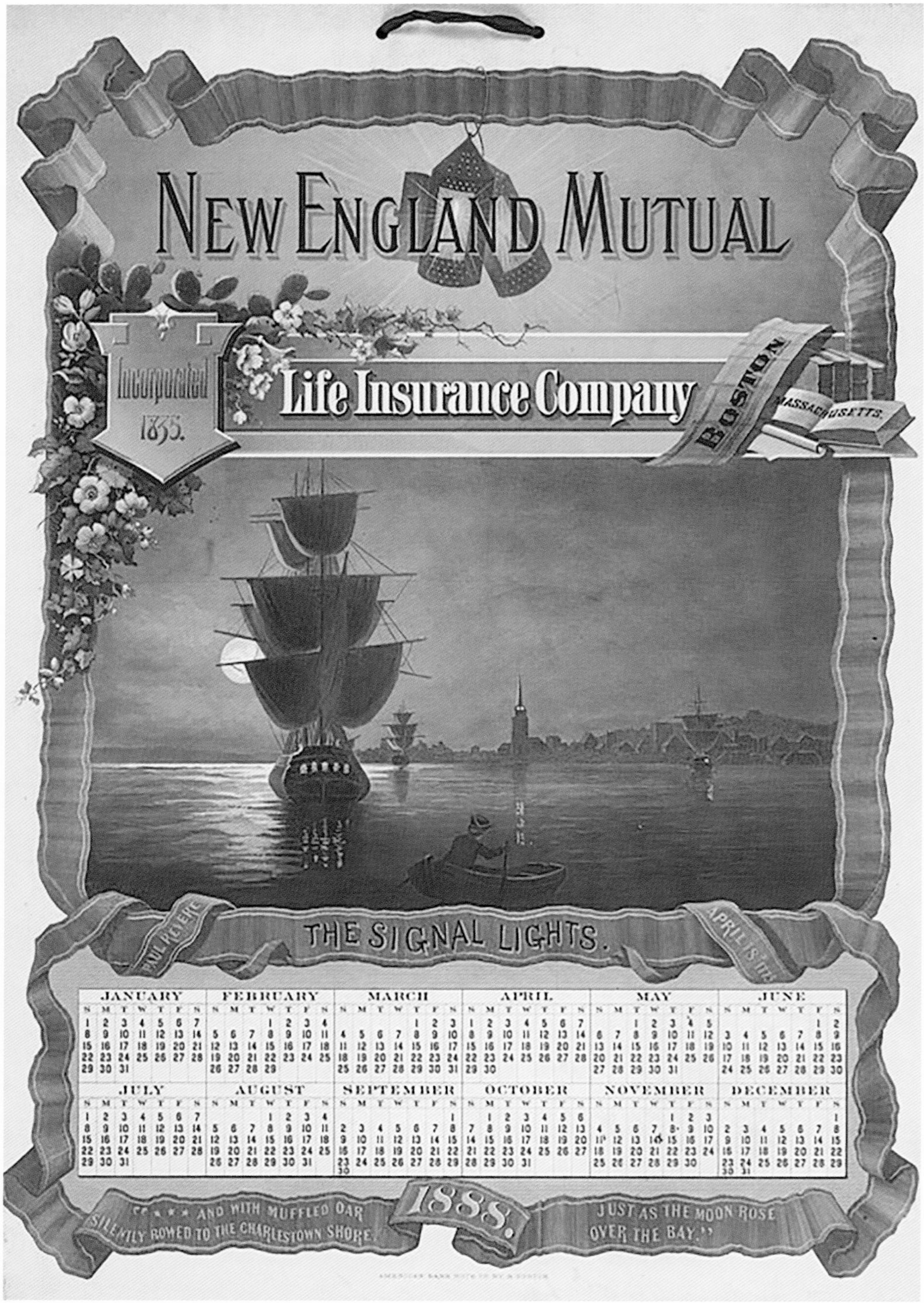

An 1888 calendar shows Revere's fateful rowboat journey. Lines from Longfellow's poem in the scroll at the bottom about the "muffled oar" and how the "moon rose over the bay" make it clear that the image was inspired by Longfellow's poem rather than what really happened that night. Artist unknown.

Chapter 3

Across the Charles

Then he said "Good night!" and with muffled oar
Silently rowed to the Charlestown shore,
Just as the moon rose over the bay,
Where swinging wide at her moorings lay
The Somerset, British man-of-war;
A phantom ship, with each mast and spar
Across the moon like a prison bar,
And a huge black hulk, that was magnified
By its own reflection in the tide.

Throughout his eighty-three years, Revere was many things—silversmith, goldsmith, coppersmith, businessman, dentist, messenger, soldier, spy, and bell maker. He was also a hunter, a pub crawler, a card player, a theatergoer, a member of five Boston social clubs, and an artist whose 1770 engraving of the Boston Massacre is familiar to every student of American history. But Revere was not a waterman. Rowing was not his thing. So on April 17, he recruited two veteran harbor hands and told them to be ready to row him the third of a mile from Boston to Charlestown. One of these men was a forty-eight-year-old boatbuilder named Joshua Bentley. He lived in the North End of Boston on Henchman's Lane, a block from the water.

Seeing Revere at his door, Bentley threw on his coat, and together the two men walked up to Lynn Street, turned right, and then made a quick left onto Hunt's Wharf. Named for the previous owner, this wharf and the surrounding houses now belonged to Bentley and his father.

Here they waited for the second operative, Thomas Richardson, an unmarried twenty-six-year-old shipbuilder. Who alerted Richardson is not known, but we do know that somewhere between his rooming house and the meeting spot at Hunt's Wharf, Richardson realized he lacked a vital piece of equipment: a piece of cloth. Why is that vital? Because, as Longfellow wrote in his poem, the rowing had to be done with muffled oars. Any grinding or creaking in the oarlocks could alert the British sailors on the *Somerset*. Richardson didn't have time to turn around and go back to his room. But he did have a girlfriend who lived on the nearby corner of Ann and North Center Streets. After a knock at the door and a hushed conversation with the girl's father, a few moments passed. Then a second-story window opened and "something white fell noiselessly to the ground." It was a woolen petticoat, tossed down by Richardson's girlfriend—and still warm from her body.

Richardson scooped up the garment

Revere Goes to Court

Usually modest, level-headed, and restrained, Paul Revere occasionally lost his cool and dished out a few left jabs. In 1761, a Boston hatter filed a complaint against Revere "for assaulting and beating" him. After a hearing, the judge found Revere guilty, fined him "six shillings, eight pence, and court costs," and ordered him "to keep ye peace and be of good behavior." He also asked two reputable citizens to put up money that would be forfeited if Revere misbehaved again. Twelve years later, in May 1773, two British customs officials "were very much abused" on a Boston street. A merchant identified Revere as one of the "principal actors." As historian Jayne Triber points out, "Revere's willingness to resort to fisticuffs surely marked him as no gentleman, but it did suggest qualities that would be useful to the patriot cause."

and made his way to Hunt's Wharf, where he joined Revere and Bentley. The three men snaked around wooden boat ribs; rusty anchors; and piles of booms, rigging, and buoys. At the head of the wharf, they ducked into Bentley's boat shed. Richardson cut up the petticoat and swaddled the oarlocks. Then all three climbed aboard, and Bentley eased his little rowboat into the Charles River.

With the younger Richardson pulling the oars, Bentley handled the tiller. Longfellow wrote that as Revere's boat neared the *Somerset*, the moon rose over the bay. On most nights, that would have been the case. But on April 18, 1775, the three patriots got lucky. A "lunar anomaly" kept the moon hanging very low in the southern sky, where its beams were blocked by Boston's many church steeples. So instead of being splashed by moonlight, the rowboat was "shrouded in the dark moon shadow," and it skimmed past the *Somerset*, unseen by any British sailors at the rail.

"I was put across [the] Charles River in a private boat," wrote Revere. According to Boston historian Carl Zellner, Revere was probably landed at Captain Orr's Wharf, a structure "visible in semi-darkness" and "well known to local watermen."

With Revere safely deposited in Charlestown, Longfellow zips us back to Boston.

Meanwhile, his friend, through alley and street
Wanders and watches with eager ears,
Till in the silence around him he hears
The muster of men at the barrack door,
The sound of arms, and the tramp of feet,
And the measured tread of the grenadiers,
Marching down to their boats on the shore.

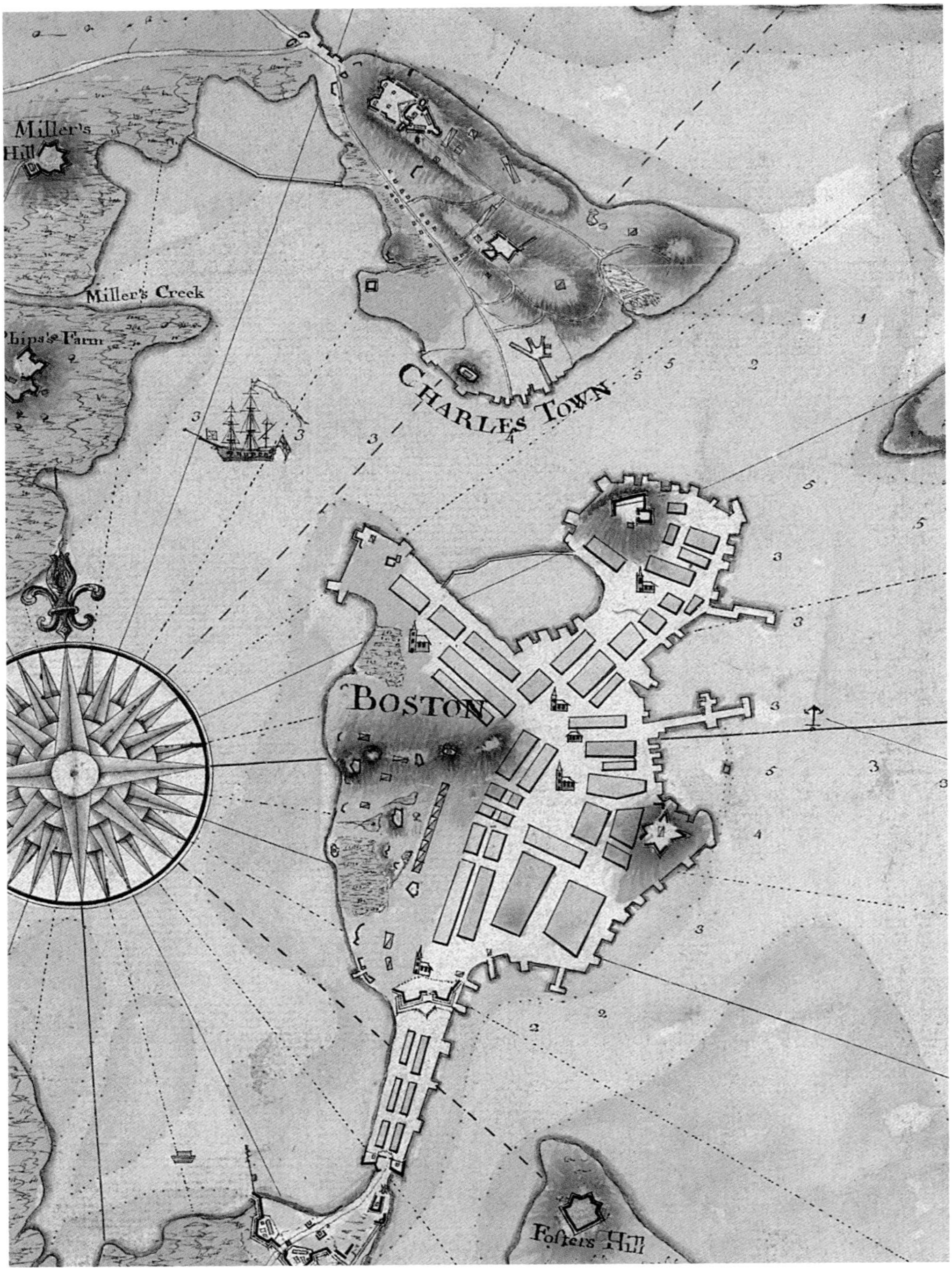

Richardson and Bentley rowed Revere across from Boston to Charlestown the night of April 18, 1775.

Do you see the flaw here? Revere's friend, John Pulling, had no reason to wander and watch, because Revere's directive—"two lanterns"—had told him everything he needed to know. Namely, the regulars were marching down to their boats and leaving Boston by water. Collar up, head down, and no time to lose, Pulling flouted General Gage's curfew, zig-zagged through Boston's alleys and streets, dodged the marching grenadiers, and made his way toward a three-story brick dwelling on the corner of Salem and Sheafe Streets.

In this house resided the only man with the key to the massive wooden door of the North Church. His name was Robert Newman. He was twenty-three years old, and he lived with his wife, two sons, and his widowed mother, who owned the place. Hard economic times had forced Newman to give up his trade as a maker of leather breeches and seek the job of groundskeeper, or sexton, at the North Church. Someone who knew him said that Newman "was a man of few words, but prompt and active, capable of doing whatever Paul Revere wished to have done."

On April 17, Revere told Newman the plan, and early the next day, Newman had gone to the church and "primed two lanterns and made them ready in the closet next to the door leading to the steeple."

It was nearly ten thirty when Pulling arrived outside the Newman house. He looked through the front window, and . . . oh no! Sitting in the parlor, hunched

Very Old Tea Leaves

John Pulling and Paul Revere both took part in the Boston Tea Party. Unlike most of the patriots, Pulling didn't bother with a disguise. Instead he wore his usual garb, including a three-cornered hat. When he returned home, his wife noticed a few tea leaves stuck in the creases of the hat. She preserved them in a small vial that was passed down to the Pulling descendants. In 1909, the tea leaves were in the possession of Mrs. Pulling's great-great-grandson. There has been no update since then, but those historic tea leaves are probably out there somewhere.

over playing cards and glasses of rum, were three British officers who were renting rooms from Newman's mother.

Now what? Pulling couldn't knock, nor could he hang around in front of the house, because the streets were filling with soldiers. Luckily for Pulling, Newman chose that moment to wander over to the window and glance into the street. Pulling flashed him a prearranged signal. Newman turned, casually took his candle, and creaked up the stairs as if to retire for the night.

Robert Newman's house, corner of Salem and Sheaffe Streets, North End, Boston, circa 1898. It is no longer there.

From a bedroom on the Sheafe Street side of the house, Newman eased open a window, climbed out, shinnied down the sloping roof, and lowered himself into the garden. Pulling was waiting. So was Thomas Barnard, Revere's third operative. Barnard was Revere's neighbor, so while nobody is certain, he could have been activated when Revere returned home from Dr. Warren's.

Pulling, Newman, and Barnard walked half a block to the North Church. Newman keyed open the big wooden door, and he and Pulling slipped inside. Barnard stayed on the steps, "watching the movement of the troops." If any soldiers got close, he would rap on the door before sprinting off.

And now, as we enter the North Church, we come to the most truthful stanza of "Paul Revere's Ride." It's truthful because Longfellow described the same climb that he himself made the day before he began writing the poem.

Give the Guy Some Credit

British commander General Thomas Gage tried to keep the British march secret. Instead of dictating his orders, Gage wrote them himself. Meat for the eight hundred regulars was grilled not in the barracks but "on a transport-ship in the harbor," far from patriot noses. Gage gave regimental commanders no details. Only the commanding officer, Lieutenant-Colonel Francis Smith, knew where the regulars were marching and why.

A little after nine o'clock at night, British officers tiptoed into various barracks. They gently shook awake soldiers and whispered to "equip themselves immediately with their arms and 36 rounds of powder and ball." Soldiers walked through the streets "with the utmost silence." A dog barked and "was instantly killed with a bayonet."

However, Boston was a tough place to keep a secret, and by ten o'clock Gage's veil of secrecy had been pierced by Dr. Warren, William Dawes, and Paul Revere.

Christ Church, more commonly known as Old North Church, in Boston's North End is where two lanterns were hung the night of April 18, 1775. It is now a museum as well.

Chapter 4

Seeing the Lights

Then he climbed to the tower of the church,
Up the wooden stairs, with stealthy tread,
To the belfry-chamber overhead,
And startled the pigeons from their perch
On the sombre rafters, that round him made
Masses and moving shapes of shade,—
Up the trembling ladder, steep and tall,
To the highest window in the wall,
Where he paused to listen and look down
A moment on the roofs of the town,
And the moonlight flowing over all.

Convincing? Yes. Full of evocative details? Yes. But here's the problem. Longfellow described only one person making the climb. Given the difficulty of carrying, lighting, and hanging two lanterns simultaneously, it's unlikely that's what actually happened. Historian Fischer believes it was a two-man operation. If he's right, here's how it all might have gone down—or, in this case, gone up.

Newman opened the closet, grabbed the lanterns, and handed one to Pulling. Using strips of leather, each man hung a lantern around his neck. Then up they went: fourteen stories and 154 steps, past the opening for

repairing the organ and past the eight bells rung many years earlier by the teenage Paul Revere and seven of his pals. Young Revere and his friends took that job so seriously that they drew up a "Bell Ringer's Agreement" in which they promised to "ring at any time . . . the warden of the church . . . shall desire it."

In the steeple, the stairway gave way to ladders. With the lanterns likely thumping against their chests, Newman and Pulling gripped the rungs of the trembling ladder. They monkeyed upward as chilly sea winds whooshed through the wooden window slats that let in the pigeons and let out the pealing of the bells.

On the highest landing, glass windows offered protection from the wind. From here, the loftiest perch in Boston, slivers of moonglow probably revealed the silhouette of the *Somerset* and the inky shoreline of Charlestown.

Undoing the leather straps, the two men knelt and placed the lanterns on the gritty wooden floor. As the windows rattled in their frames, Newman warmed his hands, then pulled the flint, the steel, and the tinderboxes from his pocket. Dragging the steel across the flint, he sent a stream of sparks into the dry tinder and lightly "blew the glowing timber into a flame." Pulling lit his candle, then Newman flared his. The men stood. Newman threw open the sash on the northwest-facing window. They leaned out. One man held a lantern in his left

Ring-a-Ding-Ding

Ringing the North Church bells was no simple task, because the church was the first in the colonies to import a set of eight bells. Each bell had a different tone, and "playing" them properly required each ringer to reach up, grab the rope, pull down hard, and "catch the rope at a precise point marked by a tuft of brightly colored wool." Flubbing the catch meant the bell would swing out too far or swing back too soon. Each bell-ringing session lasted for two hours!

The boys' "Bell Ringer's Agreement" is the only surviving document from Revere's childhood.

hand, the other in his right. The eight feet between the lanterns meant that from a distance the two beams would not appear as one. Fearful that a British sailor on the *Somerset* would spot the signal or that some "old woman would see the lights and scream, 'Fire!'" the men held the lanterns up for just a few seconds.

Thanks to Mr. Longfellow, those few seconds of lantern light turned into the most unforgettable signal in American history.

But look at what the poet did next. Instead of giving us the reaction of the Charlestown patriots who *saw* the signal, Longfellow stayed with the unnamed friend in the belfry. And after five stanzas of pulsating action, he brought the story to a sudden standstill.

Beneath, in the churchyard, lay the dead,
In their night-encampment on the hill,
Wrapped in silence so deep and still
That he could hear, like a sentinel's tread,
The watchful night-wind, as it went
Creeping along from tent to tent,
And seeming to whisper, "All is well!"
A moment only he feels the spell
Of the place and the hour, and the secret dread
Of the lonely belfry and the dead;

What's going on here? Why ten lines about a guy gazing out a window? And why all this spooky talk about the dead and the secret dread and the voice that isn't really a voice? Professor and poet Dana Gioia calls Longfellow "a master of narrative pacing" and says that by "slowing down the plot at this crucial moment, . . . [he] builds suspense." By

bringing a graveyard into the poem, Longfellow also foreshadowed the deadly battle that was fought the following day.

Okay, all that seems fair enough, but what about the tents? There were no tents in the graveyard. Professor Gioia explains that in looking down at the Copp's Hill Burying Ground, Revere's friend in the poem imagined a military encampment. That's a natural association, because in 1768, two thousand British soldiers had arrived and promptly turned Boston Common into a campsite. Extending the metaphor, the friend perceived the headstones as tents and noticed how silent the graveyard was compared to the boisterous British camp a mile away. It's so quiet, wrote Longfellow, that the friend could hear the night wind drifting among the headstones like a sentinel's tread—a simile he added to his metaphor.

Then the poet reached deep into his writer's toolkit and gave us a *third* figure of speech. He personified the night wind and sent it creeping and whispering, "All is well." Wait a second. We've got regulars on the move and a confrontation looming, but all is well? How so? Well, just like those "sleeping soldiers" once did, patriots across Middlesex County were preparing to fight for what they believed in. And the dead in the churchyard are the patriots' ghostly

Consequences

Robert Newman and John Pulling's worst fear was realized. A British sailor saw the two lanterns. A few days later, "while engaged at his duties at a funeral," Newman was arrested. When questioned, Newman said that Pulling had asked for the key to the North Church.

When soldiers arrived at the Pulling house, John's wife said she had no idea where he was. In fact, he'd been tipped off and was in the cellar, crouching under a beer butt.

The next day, Pulling and his wife boarded a skiff out of Boston. Mrs. Pulling had no intention of leaving behind the family silver, so she tied a pepperbox and cream pitcher to her hoop skirt. Both were gifts from Paul Revere.

Newman met with "cruel usage" while in jail, and according to one historian, he did not regain his freedom until George Washington arrived in Cambridge three months later and negotiated a prisoner exchange.

ancestors giving them permission—and urging them—to take up arms and challenge a mighty king.

Longfellow scholar Christoph Irmscher believes that Longfellow slowed everything down for a moment to "remind his readers that Americans have their own history, their own dead, a silent army of supporters in their struggle for independence and liberty."

Having given us a lovely "lyric moment of reflection," Longfellow then had Revere's friend snap out of his dream state and stare upriver.

Copp's Hill Burying Ground circa 1895. It is now part of Boston's Freedom Trail and open to visitors.

For suddenly all his thoughts are bent
On a shadowy something far away,
Where the river widens to meet the bay,—
A line of black that bends and floats
On the rising tide, like a bridge of boats.

This is credible. The friend in the belfry could have seen the shadowy boat parade. And yes, the British transports did, in fact, look like a bridge, because they were tied to each other (bow to stern) in strings of three or four, so the coxswains wouldn't lose their way in the dark.

With the British invasion underway, Longfellow made what Professor Gioia calls "a decisive . . . cut" and transported us from the North Church belfry to Revere on the Charlestown shore. Gioia suspects that no other nineteenth-century poet would have handled this transition so boldly.

So across the Charles River we go.

A postcard of a 1917 painting called The Midnight Ride of Paul Revere *by W. R. Leigh.*

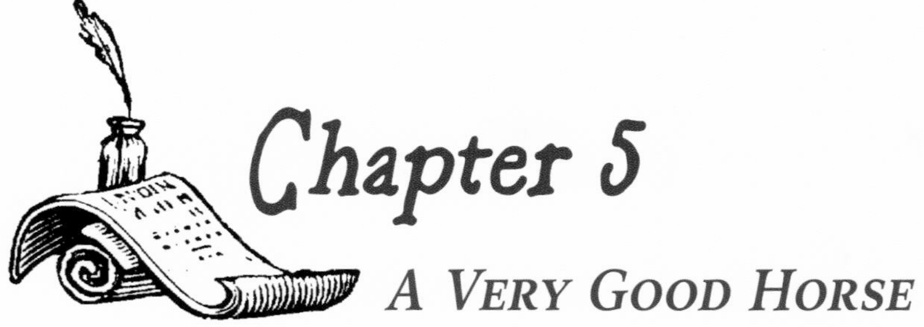

Chapter 5

A Very Good Horse

Meanwhile, impatient to mount and ride,
Booted and spurred, with a heavy stride
On the opposite shore walked Paul Revere.

Longfellow was correct. Shortly before eleven o'clock that night, Revere was booted and spurred and walking from Captain Orr's Wharf toward the center of Charlestown. And yes, he was impatient to mount and ride.

Now he patted his horse's side,

No, sorry. Revere hadn't yet met his horse. At this point, he was probably hurrying over the swing bridge that crossed the boat slip by the Charlestown town dock.

Now gazed at the landscape far and near,
Then, impetuous, stamped the earth,
And turned and tightened his saddle-girth;
But mostly he watched with eager search
The belfry-tower of the Old North Church,

As it rose above the graves on the hill,
Lonely and spectral and sombre and still.
And lo! as he looks, on the belfry's height
A glimmer, and then a gleam of light!
He springs to the saddle, the bridle he turns,

Sorry, still no horse yet. Revere was just now walking up Fish Street.

But lingers and gazes, till full on his sight
A second lamp in the belfry burns!

Wrong. Revere did no lingering and gazing, because he already knew that two lanterns would be shown. Instead, it was the patriots on the Charlestown shore who lingered and gazed.

This postcard circa 1930s or 1940s shows Paul Revere arriving in Charlestown while the lanterns are still shining from the church steeple, which isn't what really happened. Artist unknown.

What's more, by the time Revere got across the Charles River, the lanterns had already been displayed. We know this because when Revere arrived in Charlestown, his patriot pals told him that they had seen the two signals. Revere told the Charlestown men "what was acting," and then, as he put it, "I . . . went to git me a horse." It was roughly an hour after his meeting with Dr. Warren when Revere finally put his foot in the stirrup and sprang to the saddle.

Up Graves Lane he trotted, before turning right onto High Street. "I set off upon a very good horse," wrote Revere. The horse's name was Brown Beauty, and according to historian Fischer, she was "an excellent specimen of a New England saddlehorse—big, strong, and very fast."

Revere recalled, "It was then about 11 o'clock, and very pleasant" and, "The moon shone bright."

In 1775, Charlestown, like Boston, was a peninsula. The Charles River lay to the south, and the Mystic River to the north. Just past Charlestown Neck was the common, a dreary landscape of scrub, shrubs, and clay pits. Revere crossed Charlestown Common and raced down the road that forked southwest toward Cambridge. This was the shortest route to Lexington.

Suddenly Brown Beauty slowed, and up popped her ears. Revere wrote that he peered ahead and could make out "two [British] officers on horse back" under a tree, "in a narrow part of the road." He got near enough "to see their holsters and cockades."

The soldiers spoke. One moved slowly toward the center of the road,

Not a Pretty Sight

Just past Charlestown Neck, Revere rode by a gruesome landmark: a human skeleton, still in chains and locked in a rusted, iron cage. It was the remains of an enslaved person named Mark. Twenty years earlier, Mark had poisoned his abusive master. After he was hanged, his body was locked in a cage. His skinless skull and bleached bones served as a grim warning to any enslaved person contemplating murder.

while the other spun toward Revere and accelerated. Revere jerked on Brown Beauty's reins, wheeled her around, and surged back toward Charlestown Neck. The race was on! Time for Brown Beauty to show her stuff. It was also time for Longfellow to leave behind his more lyrical moments and return to some rip-roaring action. (Although Longfellow changed Brown Beauty from a she to a he.)

A hurry of hoofs in a village street,
A shape in the moonlight, a bulk in the dark,
And beneath, from the pebbles, in passing, a spark
Struck out by a steed flying fearless and fleet;
That was all! And yet, through the gloom and the light,
The fate of a nation was riding that night;
And the spark struck out by that steed, in his flight,
Kindled the land into flame with its heat.

Revere wrote that he took off "upon a full gallop for Mystic Road." At the intersection, he careered hard to the left and headed northward. The British officer who gave chase lost ground and saw that the only way to overtake the rebel rider was to go off-road and slice diagonally across the murky moonscape of the common. The officer promptly rode into a clay pond and got stuck in the caramel ooze. Horse and rider resembled a military statue in a city park.

Revere's escape extended his ride by a mile, but it turned out to be a fortunate detour because the Mystic Road was empty of British patrols.

Longfellow wrote a picturesque (and accurate) account of Revere's riverside gallop and Brown Beauty's charge up and over the 120-foot-high Winter Hill.

He has left the village and mounted the steep,
And beneath him, tranquil and broad and deep,
Is the Mystic, meeting the ocean tides;
And under the alders, that skirt its edge,
Now soft on the sand, now loud on the ledge,
Is heard the tramp of his steed as he rides.

Around quarter after eleven that night, Brown Beauty raced past a mansion belonging to a loyalist named Isaac Royall, who owned all the land from Winter Hill to Medford. Thanks to historian and archaeologist Alexandra Chan, we know that Royall commissioned several silver pieces from Revere, including a three-gallon punch bowl that Royall kept filled with rum. So it's likely that as Revere crested the hill, he was flying past some of his own gleaming creations.

Revere followed the Mystic Road for four miles and clopped over a wooden bridge.

It was twelve by the village clock
When he crossed the bridge into Medford town.

If Revere left Charlestown around eleven (as he wrote), and if a galloping horse averages about twenty-five miles per hour (as most do), it was probably closer to twenty past eleven when he rode into Medford, population 800, a village noted at the time for its rum distilleries.

He heard the crowing of the cock,
And the barking of the farmer's dog,
And felt the damp of the river fog,
That rises after the sun goes down.

Yo Ho Ho!

Rum is made from fermented molasses and was invented in the West Indies in the seventeenth century. It soon became the most popular drink in the colonies, with the average drinker downing about four gallons a year. The rum from Captain Isaac Hall's distillery was said to be strong enough to make "a rabbit bite a bulldog."

Do cocks crow at night? Don't they cock-a-doodle-do only to signal dawn? Actually, chicken owners will tell you that roosters crow at all hours. Sure, they may crow to announce the sunrise, but they also crow to alert hens to a potential threat. The clopping of Revere's horse may have seemed like such a threat.

It was in Medford that Revere began to improvise. Recall that Dr. Warren said nothing about spreading the alarm to every Middlesex village and farm—but that's exactly what Revere began to do. Backtracking to 23 High Street, he dismounted and pounded on the door of Isaac Hall, the thirty-nine-year-old captain of the Medford minutemen.

If you're wondering how Revere knew where Hall lived, remember that Revere had been carrying messages to patriot leaders near and far since the Boston Tea Party in December 1773. As a result, he was the link between the many colonial committees and congresses that had formed to protest both excessive British taxes and King George's 1774 decision to close Boston Harbor as punishment for the Tea Party. Journalist Malcolm Gladwell writes that by April 1775, Revere had the thickest address book in Boston, and whenever he arrived in a town, he knew exactly "whose door to knock on [and] who the local militia leader was."

Isaac Hall immediately triggered the local alarm. Within minutes, Medford resounded with an ominous cacophony of "gunshots, the beating of drums, and the ringing of bells."

Medford's fifty-nine minutemen reported to the town's meeting house, where Hall announced they would leave for Concord at first light.

One man was too impatient to wait until dawn. Right after the meeting, Reverend Edward Brooks went back to his house, filled a bag with provisions, threw a saddle on his horse, grabbed his musket, and rode off. Another Medford man jumped on his horse and carried the alarm east to Malden, where another man saddled up and rode to Chelsea, on the coast.

Here we see the beginning of the Revere ripple effect. As soon as patriot leaders in one town got the alarm, designated messengers were sent off to alert nearby towns. Longfellow's poem would have us believe that spreading the alarm was a one-man show. In fact, upwards of thirty alarm riders sprinted across Middlesex County that night. This was community organizing at its best.

And sometimes no organizing was necessary. Sometimes the ripple happened spontaneously. For instance, after leaving Hall's, Revere rode through Medford Square, where he had a chance meeting with a stranger named Martin Herrick. This young doctor had spent the day studying with Dr. Simon Tufts Jr., brother of Samuel Tufts, another midnight rider. When Revere struck up a conversation, he found out that Herrick was on his way home to Lynn End, about fifteen miles to the northeast. Once Revere determined that Herrick was a patriot, he told him of the British march, and Herrick said he'd sound the alarm in Lynn End as well as in the two towns (Stoneham and Reading) along his route.

Revere followed High Street through West Medford, again crossed the Mystic River, and continued southwest to Menotomy. The town's name is an Algonquian word meaning "swift running water." Though Longfellow named three other towns in his poem, he didn't mention Menotomy. It can be a hard word for some people to pronounce. The British had no idea how to say it. They called it "Monotony" or "Anatomy." In 1867, the city changed its name to Arlington. In Menotomy, Revere woke minutemen officers Solomon Bowman and Benjamin Locke, both of whom went out to rouse their neighbors.

This map shows the routes of 22 different midnight riders (including Revere and Dawes) who helped spread the word across the Massachusetts countryside the night of April 18 and 19, 1775.

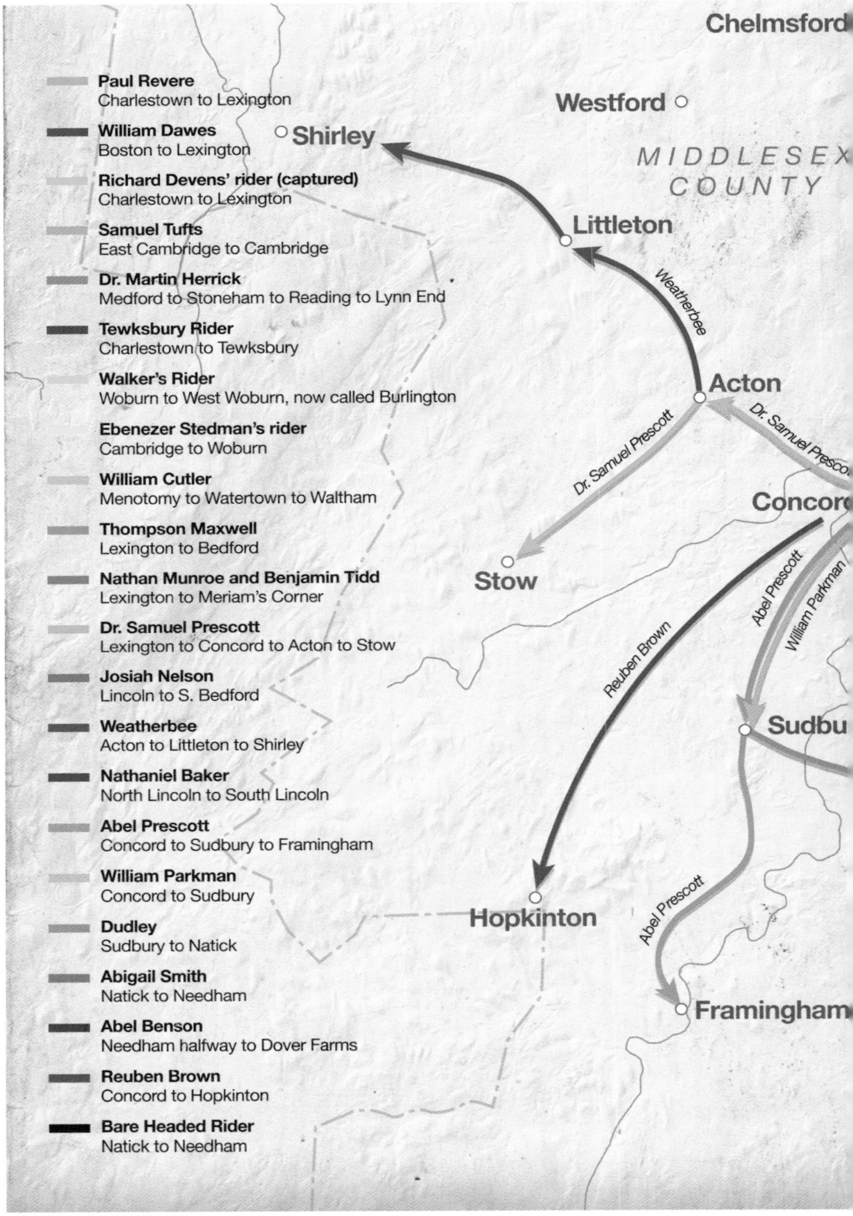

Paul Revere
Charlestown to Lexington
William Dawes
Boston to Lexington
Richard Devens' rider (captured)
Charlestown to Lexington
Samuel Tufts
East Cambridge to Cambridge
Dr. Martin Herrick
Medford to Stoneham to Reading to Lynn End
Tewksbury Rider
Charlestown to Tewksbury
Walker's Rider
Woburn to West Woburn, now called Burlington
Ebenezer Stedman's rider
Cambridge to Woburn
William Cutler
Menotomy to Watertown to Waltham
Thompson Maxwell
Lexington to Bedford
Nathan Munroe and Benjamin Tidd
Lexington to Meriam's Corner
Dr. Samuel Prescott
Lexington to Concord to Acton to Stow
Josiah Nelson
Lincoln to S. Bedford
Weatherbee
Acton to Littleton to Shirley
Nathaniel Baker
North Lincoln to South Lincoln
Abel Prescott
Concord to Sudbury to Framingham
William Parkman
Concord to Sudbury
Dudley
Sudbury to Natick
Abigail Smith
Natick to Needham
Abel Benson
Needham halfway to Dover Farms
Reuben Brown
Concord to Hopkinton
Bare Headed Rider
Natick to Needham

Chelmsford
Westford
Shirley
MIDDLESEX COUNTY
Littleton
Weatherbee
Acton
Dr. Samuel Prescott
Stow
Abel Prescott
William Parkman
Reuben Brown
Hopkinton
Framingham

One neighbor—Abel Locke—didn't need rousing. He was an elderly shoemaker who, with help from his wife, was already busy melting pewter dishes and forming the molten liquid into musket balls. And they were hardly the only ones repurposing their kitchenware. Men, women,

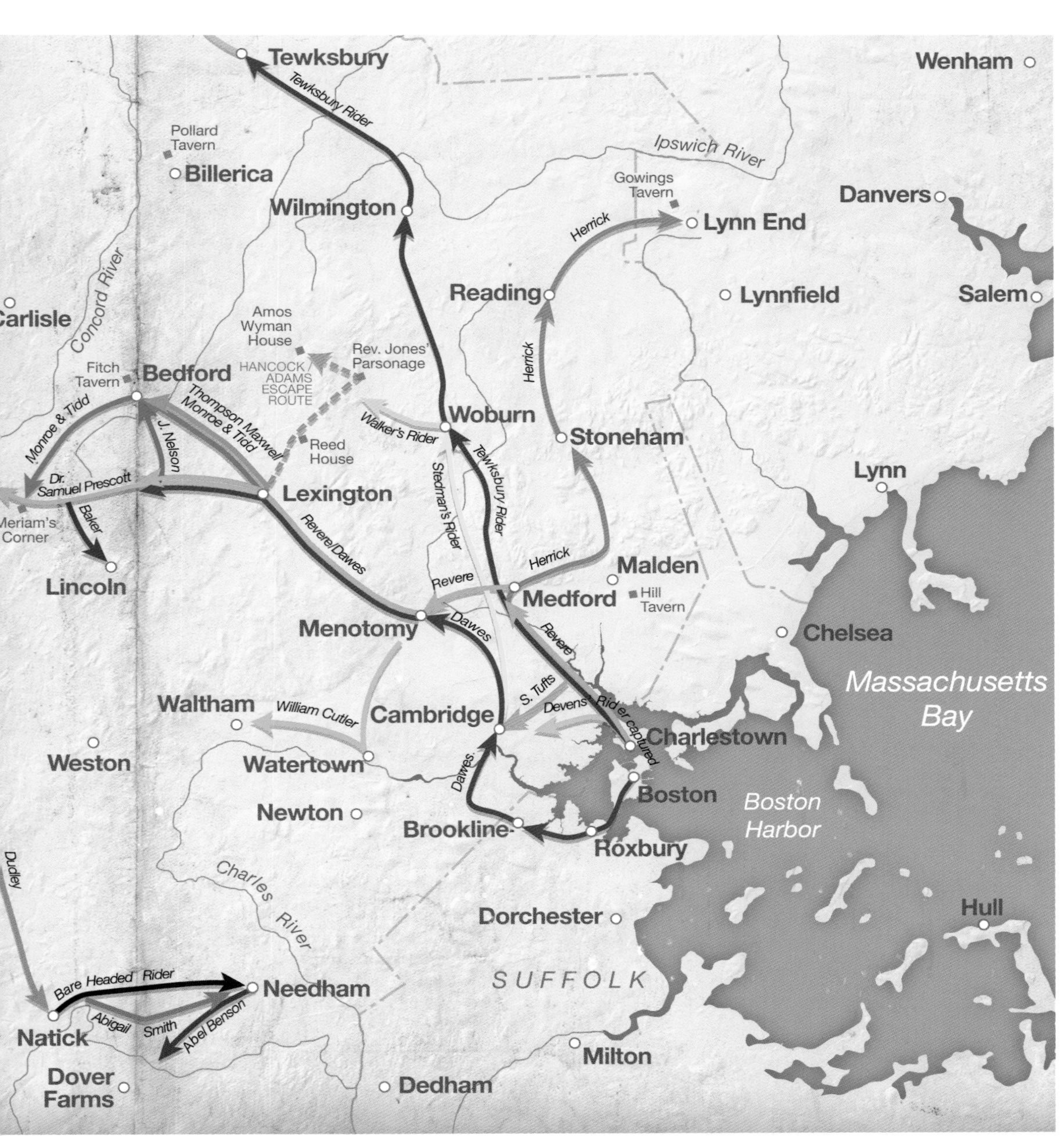

and older children all across Middlesex County were using fireplace tools and elementary physics to add to the patriot arsenal.

And then, just in case you forgot about the ticking clock, the next section of the poem will jog your memory.

Paul Revere is so popular, he and his ride are depicted in countless images. This one is from the early 1940s by an unknown artist.

Chapter 6

Hello, Mr. Dawes

It was one by the village clock,
When he galloped into Lexington.
He saw the gilded weathercock
Swim in the moonlight as he passed,
And the meeting-house windows, blank and bare,
Gaze at him with a spectral glare,
As if they already stood aghast
At the bloody work they would look upon.

Longfellow was off by about an hour. Historians agree it was closer to midnight when Revere galloped into Lexington, a farming town of 750 people, 590 cows, 300 sheep and goats, 220 swine, 130 horses, 118 houses, seven shoe shops, six elementary schools, three tanners, two doctors (a father and son), two taverns, two blacksmiths, and one tailor. Extended families were the rule. The 181 landowning taxpayers (all men) included fourteen Munroes (or Munros), ten Harringtons (or Herringtons), nine Reeds, eight Smiths, and five Parkers, including forty-six-year-old John Parker, the commander of the Lexington militia.

Brown Beauty was likely exhausted, steaming, and foam-flecked as Revere guided her past the meeting house, turned right onto the Bedford

Buckman Tavern in Lexington, Massachusetts, where Revere, Lowell, Adams, and Hancock "refreshed themselves" the night of April 18 and 19, 1775. It is now a museum.

Road, and headed toward Reverend Jonas Clarke's safe house, where John Hancock and Samuel Adams were lying low.

The place was packed. Hancock and Adams had taken over the parlor. Upstairs in one bedroom were Hancock's aunt Lydia and his fiancée, Dolly. Across the hall were Reverend and Mrs. Clarke and their infant daughter. Crammed into a third bedroom were eight more Clarke children, who ranged in age from five to fifteen. There was no room for Hancock's personal secretary, John Lowell, so he stayed down the road at Buckman Tavern, which had an upstairs bunkroom.

As Revere neared the Clarke house, armed men emerged from the shadows. A local security force had assembled earlier in the evening, after a Lexington man, returning home from Boston, reported seeing British officers on the road. The leader of the security group was a tavern

owner named William Munroe. He recalled later that Paul Revere rode up and asked to be allowed to enter the Clarke house. Munroe said everyone had gone to bed, and they didn't wish to be disturbed by any noise.

"Noise!" exclaimed Revere. "You'll soon have a *noise* that will disturb you all. The British troops are on their march."

Upon hearing this, Munroe "permitted him to pass."

Revere knocked on the door, and Reverend Clarke opened an upstairs window and "inquired who was there." Revere either didn't hear the question or else ignored it. He answered that "he wished to see Mr. Hancock." Clarke couldn't see Revere and didn't recognize his voice. He replied that he "did not like to admit people into his house, at that time of night, without first knowing their business." Hancock did recognize the voice, however. He opened the parlor window and shouted, "Come in, Revere; we are not afraid of you."

Revere entered and gave Hancock the written warning from Dr. Warren. After reading it, Hancock walked outside and headed down the road to Buckman Tavern, where he ordered the Lexington town bell rung. The thing weighed 463 pounds, and after the bell ringers were summoned, it didn't take more than a few clangs to alarm the local militia.

What's the Difference?

Minutemen and militiamen were two different colonial military forces. Every able-bodied man between the ages of sixteen and sixty was expected to serve in his town's militia. The only exceptions were clergymen, college students, professors, the mentally incompetent, and conscientious objectors. Militiamen drilled on a regular basis, but they were paid only if they fought in a battle outside the boundaries of their town.

About a quarter of militiamen were chosen by their company commanders to be minutemen. This elite force consisted of men who were hardy, reliable, and usually under the age of thirty. They were better equipped, better trained, and were paid to drill. Whenever their fellow citizens were threatened, minutemen were the first to muster and march.

Revere asked about Mr. Dawes and was told he had not arrived. "I related the story of the two [British] officers," wrote Revere, "and supposed that [Dawes] must have been stopped, as he ought to have been there before me."

Half an hour later came the sound of hoofbeats. Revere went outside, and lo and behold, there was Dawes cantering up the Bedford Road. Earlier at the Boston town gate, Dawes had put on a floppy hat and played the part of a country bumpkin. The British guards suspected no mischief and waved him on through. Dawes may have been the last person permitted to exit Boston that night.

Having ridden through Roxbury, Brookline, and Brighton, the tanner had followed a route four miles longer than Revere's. It's likely that Dawes also stopped briefly at Stedman's Tavern in Cambridge to give the alarm to Captain Ebenezer Stedman, who then sent another rider north to Woburn.

When Revere explained that Dawes was another one of Dr. Warren's riders, Munroe and his men lowered their guns. Dawes dismounted and handed Samuel Adams a duplicate letter from Dr. Warren. Having completed phase one of their mission, Revere and Dawes rode back down the Bedford Road and joined Hancock and Lowell at Buckman Tavern.

"We refreshed ourselves," wrote Revere. They probably enjoyed a frothy tankard of flip and nibbled a piece of bread warmed inside Mrs. Buckman's kick toaster.

It was just after one o'clock in the morning when Revere and Dawes emerged from Buckman's. The two riders would have gladly traded their

Revere's Refreshment

Flip was a hot drink served in New England taverns. It consisted of home-brewed beer, sugar, and a splash of rum. Sometimes a raw egg was added. Then the tavern owner plunged a red-hot poker called a flip iron into the mug. The heat foamed the flip and gave it a scorched flavor.

weary horses for fresh ones, but none could be found. Lexington militia commander Parker had already sent two men east to Cambridge "to gain intelligence of the motion of the troops" and two more men north to alarm Bedford. In addition, three other young men were trailing the British patrol that had ridden through Lexington (toward Concord) four hours earlier. Before April 19 was even an hour old, five towns (Charlestown, Medford, Cambridge, Menotomy, and Lexington) had been alarmed, and more patriot riders were on their way to Malden, Stoneham, Reading, Woburn, Bedford, and Concord.

Follow the Woodpecker

On the night of April 18, 1775, Ebenezer Stedman's rider left Cambridge and alarmed Loammi Baldwin, the militia commander in Woburn. When not engaged in military pursuits, Baldwin was a civil engineer. In 1784, he was surveying land for the Middlesex Canal between the Merrimack River and Boston Harbor. In Wilmington, he saw "woodpeckers flying repeatedly to a certain tree." Curious, Baldwin wandered over, picked an apple off the ground, took a bite, and . . . eureka! The next spring, he cut off a few branches and planted a row of trees near his house. With its "excellent flavor," the Baldwin apple was soon the most popular fruit in New England.

Revere and Dawes mounted their horses and turned westward. Behind them, armed men made their way to Lexington Common, while local women and children, eager to safeguard their silver, hid valuables in swamps, hollow tree trunks, and well buckets.

At William Munroe's tavern, Mrs. Munroe began making bread, even though tears clouded her eyes and dripped into the flour. "I feared I should have no husband when the next mixing came," she recalled. Longfellow's poem says that "the fate of a nation was riding that night." So, too, were the individual fates of folks like Mr. and Mrs. Munroe.

AT THIS POINT,
ON THE OLD CONCORD ROAD AS IT THEN WAS,
ENDED THE MIDNIGHT RIDE OF
PAUL REVERE.

HE HAD, AT ABOUT TWO O'CLOCK OF THE MORNING OF APRIL 19, 1775, THE NIGHT BEING CLEAR AND THE MOON IN ITS THIRD QUARTER, GOT THUS FAR ON HIS WAY FROM LEXINGTON TO CONCORD, ALARMING THE INHABITANTS AS HE WENT, WHEN HE AND HIS COMPANIONS, WILLIAM DAWES, OF BOSTON, AND DR. SAMUEL PRESCOTT, OF CONCORD, WERE SUDDENLY HALTED BY A BRITISH PATROL, WHO HAD STATIONED THEMSELVES AT THIS BEND OF THE ROAD. DAWES, TURNING BACK, MADE HIS ESCAPE. PRESCOTT, CLEARING THE STONE WALL, AND FOLLOWING A PATH KNOWN TO HIM THROUGH THE LOW GROUND, REGAINED THE HIGHWAY AT A POINT FURTHER ON, AND GAVE THE ALARM AT CONCORD. REVERE TRIED TO REACH THE NEIGHBORING WOOD, BUT WAS INTERCEPTED BY A PARTY OF OFFICERS ACCOMPANYING THE PATROL, DETAINED AND KEPT IN ARREST. PRESENTLY HE WAS CARRIED BY THE PATROL BACK TO LEXINGTON. THERE RELEASED, AND THAT MORNING JOINED HANCOCK AND ADAMS.

THREE MEN OF LEXINGTON, SANDERSON, BROWN AND LORING, STOPPED AT AN EARLIER HOUR OF THE NIGHT BY THE SAME PATROL, WERE ALSO TAKEN BACK WITH REVERE.

This plaque stands at the site where the British briefly captured Revere the night of April 19, 1775. It's located in Minute Man National Park on the Battle Road Trail, just off North Great Road in Lincoln, Massachusetts.

Chapter 7

TROUBLE

**Sorry, dear reader, I have to confide
that Longfellow skipped this part of the ride.**

It's unfortunate that Longfellow left the next part out, because what happened just west of Buckman Tavern is critical to understanding how events unfolded.

Before Revere and Dawes cleared the Lexington town line, they suddenly had company.

The Boston men didn't recognize their fellow traveler, but they could see that he was young, well dressed, and well mounted. The three riders reined up and introduced themselves as the clock ticked toward one fifteen in the morning.

The country dandy was Samuel Prescott, a doctor from Concord. He had been canoodling with his fiancée in Lexington and was now on his way home. At first Revere and Dawes didn't divulge the nature of their mission. Instead they asked the doctor a few leading questions. When Prescott's answers revealed that he, too, was "a Son of Liberty," Revere told him why he and Dawes were heading for Concord.

Hearing about the British march, the doctor offered to help spread the alarm. He said he'd accompany Revere or Dawes to every house, because the people on the road knew him "and would give . . . more

credit" to the warning. The Boston men were fine with that, so at the next house, Prescott and Dawes dismounted, walked to a door, knocked, and shouted a warning. The two men heard footsteps. A latch clicked and Nathaniel Baker, age twenty-eight, opened the door. Dr. Prescott was surprised. Having cared for members of the Baker family, the doctor knew that Nathaniel still lived on his father's farm a few miles away, in the southern part of Lincoln. It turned out that Baker, like Prescott, was on a late-night "errand of love," and his girlfriend, Elizabeth Taylor, happened to live near the Lexington-Lincoln line. When Baker heard about the marching regulars, he bid Lizzie good night, put on his coat, saddled up, and galloped south to rouse his father, his four brothers, and his brother-in-law. Prescott likely warned Miss Taylor to stay inside.

Just past the Bull Tavern sat a cluster of farmhouses a few paces north of the road. In all three farmsteads lived people named Nelson. Prescott and Dawes angled toward the first Nelson house, and Revere continued toward the second until Brown Beauty picked up a danger signal and slowed. Revere squinted down the roadway and saw two men on horseback. It was no mystery who they were or what they intended.

Swiveling in his saddle, Revere called back to his fellow riders, who galloped toward him. He pointed out the British soldiers and barked, "There are two, and we will have them."

Dawes and Prescott didn't hesitate. The three patriots charged. In full gallop, the doctor turned around his riding whip and prepared to whack his way past the two soldiers.

Suddenly, from a grove of roadside trees, four more British soldiers appeared and converged on the alarm riders. One pointed his gun at Revere

"I Do"

Not long after Dr. Prescott (and the British regulars) interrupted their tryst, Nathaniel Baker and Elizabeth Taylor decided to tie the knot. They were married in 1776.

and shouted, "God damn you, stop! If you go an inch farther, you are a dead man." The three patriots yanked their reins, whirled their horses around, and searched for an opening. There was none. The soldiers had them boxed in. One soldier dismounted and walked to the fence on the north side of the road, where he lifted and tossed aside the three wooden slats. The patriots were herded through the opening into Jacob Foster's pasture.

The only known image of William Dawes is a portrait by John Johnston. It is in the Evanston History Center, Evanston, Illinois.

Barely a few yards into the thick grass, Prescott spotted a breach in the circle of soldiers. He turned to Revere and whispered, "Put on." Prescott spurred his horse, and shot the gap. Two soldiers wheeled around and went after him. Revere seized the moment and bolted in the opposite direction. Then Dawes made his move—a 180-degree turn back toward the road.

Prescott raced northwest through the pasture, jumped his agile horse over a low stone wall, dashed into a murky thicket, and got clean away. Dawes reached the roadway, spun his horse eastward, and giddyupped back toward Lexington. After a mile, his two pursuers gave up.

As for Revere, his options were limited. Unlike Prescott, he was not familiar with the off-road farm paths. Besides that, Brown Beauty had already outraced one British patrol, and she was too played out for another high-speed chase or any wall jumping. Revere steered her toward the woodland at the bottom of the pasture "intending when [he] reached

that" to jump off his horse "and run afoot" through the evergreens. But as soon as Revere neared the tree line, "out started six officers" all on horseback and all pointing their pistols at Revere. They rode over, seized Revere's bridle, grabbed the reins from his hands and ordered him to dismount, which he did. One of the soldiers asked Revere if he "was an express." ("Express" was another word for an alarm rider.)

"I answered in the affirmative," Revere wrote.

The soldier asked Revere where he had come from.

"I came out of Boston an hour after your troops had come out," said Revere, who couldn't help needling the regulars, telling them they "would miss their aim."

The interrogator claimed their aim was to find soldiers who had deserted the British camp in Boston. "I told him I knew better," wrote Revere. "I knew what they were after, [and] I had alarmed the country all the way up . . . and I should have 500 men there soon."

This was, of course, wishful thinking, but it unsettled the soldiers. They spoke among themselves. Then the interrogator said, "Sir, may I crave your name?"

"My name is Revere."

"What? Paul Revere?"

"Yes."

When the soldiers realized that the rebels' favorite courier was in front of them, they let fly with all kinds of foul language. They "abused me much," wrote Revere.

Rewriting History

In his handwritten 1798 letter to Jeremy Belknap, Revere wrote that when he saw the regulars in the roadway near Lincoln, he shouted to Dawes and Prescott, "There are two and we will have them." But Revere or Belknap (or a third person) crossed out those words, and Revere's exhortation does not appear in the published version. That suggests that twenty-three years after Revere's ride, Whig leaders were still expunging from official records any references to patriots initiating hostilities.

One of the soldiers then spurred his horse up toward the road and returned with commanding officer Major Edward Mitchell of the British Fifth Regiment.

Mitchell "clapped his pistol to my head," wrote Revere, "called me by name, and told me he was going to ask me some questions, and if I did not give him true answers, he would blow my brains out."

An indignant Revere replied that of course he would tell Mitchell the truth, but then he promptly repeated the bluff that five hundred angry colonists would soon be descending on the little detachment of regulars.

Mitchell ordered Revere searched for weapons. A pat-down revealed nothing. Good thing, too. Had Revere been packing a pistol, his night might have ended differently.

Mitchell told Revere to get back on Brown Beauty. "When I had mounted," wrote Revere, "the Major rode up to me and . . . said, 'By God, sir, you are not to ride with reins,' and [he] gave them to an officer upon my right to lead me."

Major Mitchell then ordered four "countrymen" out of the bushes.

This was Revere's first indication that he wasn't the only prisoner. The others were a local peddler with only one hand and the trio from Lexington who, five hours earlier, had set out to follow the British patrol toward Concord.

One of the Lexington men, a cabinetmaker named Elijah Sanderson, said that during his detention the soldiers "inquired where Hancock and Adams were." Sanderson reported that he gave the soldiers evasive answers. Revere didn't mention being asked about Hancock and Adams, but he did say that Major Mitchell asked him "many more . . . particular" questions. No doubt his answers were just as evasive.

According to Sanderson, it was "a quarter past two o'clock" in the morning when they all went back up to the road and mounted horses. With the patriots bunched in the middle, surrounded by the soldiers,

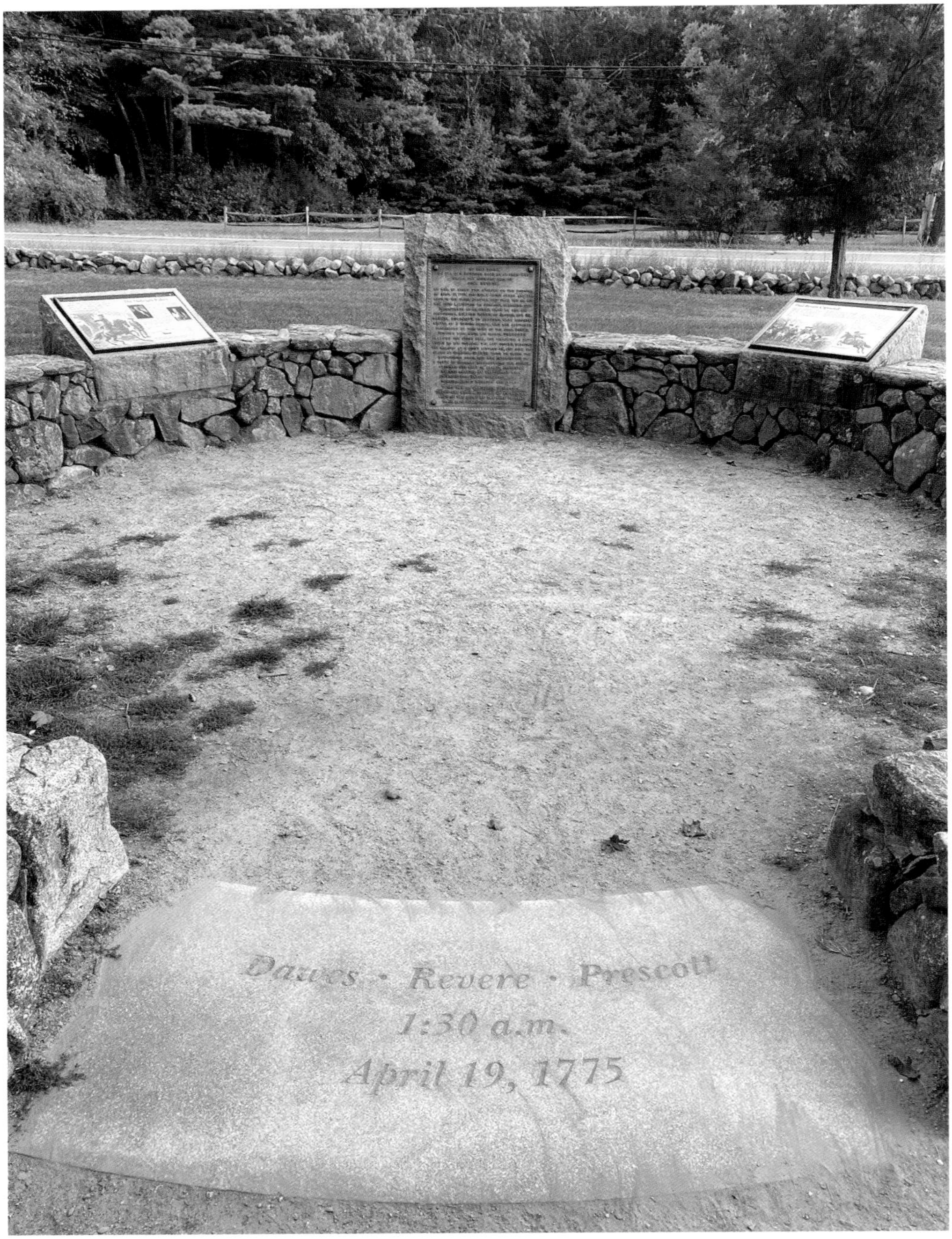

Paul Revere Capture Site, complete with plaque (shown close-up on page 48), information panels, and an engraved stone commemorating that Dawes, Revere, and Prescott were stopped together at 1:30 a.m. on April 19, 1775.

they headed toward Lexington at a "pretty smart" clip. During the ride, Revere said, he was often insulted by the soldiers, who called him a "damned rebel" and told him he was in a "critical situation."

When they neared Lexington, they heard "a gun fired."

Mitchell ordered a halt and told the three Lexington men and the one-handed peddler to dismount. One of the British officers "cut the bridles and saddles off the horses, drove them away, and told the men they might go about their business." The four locals vanished into the night. Revere asked if he, too, might be dismissed, but the major refused. "When we got within sight of the meeting-house," wrote Revere, "we heard a volley of guns fired" outside Buckman Tavern. This explosion was simply militiamen honoring a local custom: no loaded guns inside the tavern. But the volley seemed to confirm Revere's threat that a large patriot force was gathering.

Major Mitchell called another halt, rode over to his sergeant, "and asked if his horse was tired." When the sergeant answered yes, Mitchell pointed to Revere and said, "Take that man's horse." Revere dismounted. The sergeant cut the bridle and saddle off his tired horse and shooed it away. He climbed atop Brown Beauty. "They told me they should make use of my horse for the night," wrote Revere, and they all "rode off, towards Cambridge."

Now imagine you're Longfellow, writing an epic poem about a fearless American hero. Having read Revere's published account, you know that he escaped a British dragnet near Cambridge. You know that he "alarmed almost every house 'till [he] got to Lexington." But you also know that your hero was captured three miles short of Concord. I don't know what you would do, but we know what Longfellow did. He ignored it.

Old North Bridge at sunset in Minute Man National Park in Concord, Massachusetts. There have been several bridges over time. This replica was built in 1956 and restored in 2005.

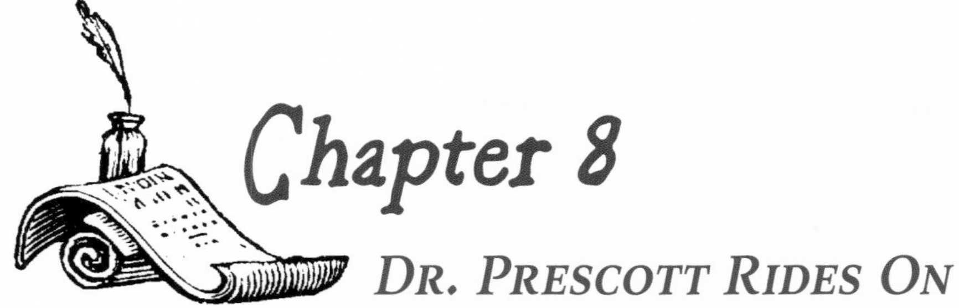

Chapter 8

Dr. Prescott Rides On

It was two by the village clock,
When he came to the bridge in Concord town.

Of all Longfellow's fictions, this is the most flagrant. At two by the village clock, Revere stood in a cow pasture with a gun to his head. At two thirty he watched Brown Beauty disappear down the road. The best thing we can say about this stanza is that Longfellow gave us the right action but the wrong guy.

The right guy was Dr. Prescott. After his wall-jumping, branch-snapping, twig-crunching detour, he emerged from the woods behind a blacksmith shop in the town of Lincoln. Tapping on the back window of the shop, Prescott awakened an enslaved woman named Sukey. After hearing Prescott's warning, Sukey ran next door to wake the shop's owner, forty-year-old Samuel Hartwell, a member of the Lincoln minutemen.

Prescott then raced to Concord, where he alerted the sentry, who rang the town bell. Up near the North Bridge, John Buttrick sprang out of bed. He was a farmer, militia leader, North Bridge repairman, and fourth-generation Concordian. Buttrick called to his sixteen-year-old son and namesake, "John, the bell's a-ringing; jump up, load your pistols, take your fife; we'll start immediately for the village."

In the meantime, Prescott had reversed course and ridden back to his father's house just east of Concord Center. Samuel's dad, Abel Prescott Sr.,

was also a doctor, as was Samuel's younger brother Abel Jr. Since all three doctors made house calls, the family was the only one in Concord with three saddle horses. The Prescotts concluded that Abel Jr. would ride southwest to alert Sudbury and Framingham, while Samuel, on a fresh horse, would gallop westward to Acton and Stow. The warnings delivered by the Prescott brothers spurred other riders to carry the alarm northwest to Littleton and southeast to Natick.

That the alarm kept spreading so quickly and methodically was no fluke. Massachusetts colonists had begun developing a communication web nearly one hundred years before, in 1676. Why then? Because a year earlier, several different Native American leaders had concluded that their tribes could no longer coexist with the thousands of land-hungry (and often violent) settlers fanning out from Boston and spilling into the Massachusetts (and Rhode Island) countryside. To defend their villages, their customs, their hunting grounds, and their sacred burial sites, four groups of Native Americans (the Wampanoag, Nipmuc, Narragansett, and Pocumtuck) teamed up and carried out raids in the Massachusetts towns of Deerfield, Northfield, Springfield, Hatfield, Medfield, Groton, Mendon, Weymouth, Worcester, Chelmsford, and Plymouth. Colonial leaders realized the need for a town-to-town warning system. Over the years, their communication methods continued to evolve. By 1775, the patriots utilized not just bells, drums, gunshots, and riders, but also trumpet blasts and bonfires. This ninety-nine-year-old network was so effective that word about the British march traveled thirty-two miles (to the New Hampshire border!) before the regulars had even sloshed through the creeks of Cambridge.

Back in Concord, both minutemen and militiamen gathered at Wright's Tavern, while Mrs. Wright hid the church communion silver in soap barrels. John Buttrick Sr. was second in command of the Concord militia, and as soon as he arrived at Wright's Tavern, he took charge and

ordered the men to go help the townspeople either cart off or tuck away all military supplies. That included not only guns, musket balls, and gunpowder, but also the whole kit and caboodle of eighteenth-century warfare: tents, cloth, canteens, plates, pots, peas, beans, beef, butter, flour, fish, rice, rum, raisins, linen, oatmeal, shovels, more fish, harnesses, wine from Spain, wine from Portugal, pickaxes, billhooks, hatchets, crowbars, wheelbarrows, iron pots, iron musket worms, salt, wooden spoons, cutting boards, matches, candles, cooking oil, molasses, medicine chests, and yes . . . even more fish! How much fish, exactly? Try seventeen thousand pounds! That's right, folks, eight and a half tons of dried and salted cod. Kudos to Concord blacksmith Elisha Jones, up on Monument Street, for piling it in his cellar and in his shed. He stored every pound of that cod *plus* twenty-five barrels of beef!

Elsewhere around Concord, men, women, and children made armaments disappear. At his home near Concord's South Bridge, Amos Wood moved a stack of muskets into a bedroom and locked the door. On Main Street, Joseph Hosmer

Going, Going, Gone

One of the men who mustered with the Lexington militia was Prince Estabrook, an enslaved black man. In 1775, enslaved people made up about two percent of the Massachusetts population. Hancock owned people. Dr. Warren bought "a negro boy" in 1770. Samuel Adams, on the other hand, refused ownership of an enslaved woman whom his wife received as a present. "A slave cannot live in my house," he said, and through the 1770s he continued to "denounce the practice of slaveholding." Revere never owned a person either.

In 1781, a Massachusetts enslaved man named Quok Walker walked into the Worcester Court of Common Pleas and successfully sued his owner for freedom. The owner appealed. Two years later, Chief Justice William Cushing of the Massachusetts Supreme Judicial Court stated that in his opinion "the clause of the [Massachusetts] constitution which declared all men to be free and equal clearly abolished slavery." By the first federal census in 1790, there were no reported enslaved people in the state. By 1804, all the northern states had abolished slavery or passed laws to gradually do so.

and his wife stashed six half barrels of gunpowder below their attic eaves and slid musket balls under Joseph's aged mother as she lay on her feather bed.

In the northern part of town, on Barrett's Mill Road, Concord's military commander, James Barrett, had his sons plow up thirty square feet of land, bury muskets in the furrows, and cover them with dirt and manure. At the same time, Barrett's farmhands tore up a bed of sage, buried a cannon—wheels and all—and replanted the crop. Inside the house, Mrs. Barrett filled barrels with musket balls, flints, and cartridges and covered them with goose feathers. She threw remaining supplies out a second-floor window into an oxcart. When the cart could hold no more, her grandson James, age fourteen, prodded the oxen toward a swamp behind the house, where he concealed everything under pine boughs.

While this was all going on, the regulars were eleven miles east of Concord, marching through Menotomy. Hearing bells, gunshots, crying babies, and barking dogs, and seeing smoking chimneys and flickering firelight in windows, British commander Colonel Francis Smith knew that his march was no longer a secret. In response, Colonel Smith sent a rider back to Boston with an urgent message for General Gage: reinforcements may be needed. Colonel Smith ordered his second-in-command, Major John Pitcairn (of the Royal Marines), to take the 230 regulars at the head of the column and quick-march them to Concord. Once there, Pitcairn and his men were to take control of Concord's North and South Bridges and wait for Colonel Smith and the rest of the regulars to arrive.

While this British advance column forged ahead and hustled through Menotomy, Paul Revere was hoofing it back toward Lexington, lending some truth to Longfellow's next lines.

He heard the bleating of the flock,
And the twitter of birds among the trees,
And felt the breath of the morning breeze
Blowing over the meadows brown.

It was around three o'clock in the morning when Paul Revere waded through a swamp, cut across the meadows brown, and picked his way around the headstones in the Lexington burying ground. Returning to the Clarke house, he was greeted by a shocking sight: Hancock, Adams, and Lowell were sitting in the parlor!

Why had they ignored Revere's warning to scram? Turns out it was because gentlemanly John Hancock had channeled his inner warrior and told everyone he wanted to stay and fight alongside the Lexington militia. Samuel Adams couldn't leave by himself, because he had no carriage and had never learned how to ride a horse.

Over the next hour, Revere, Adams, Lowell, and Clarke had all implored Hancock to reconsider, but he just shook his head and continued oiling his pistol and buffing his sword. Hancock's aunt Lydia and his fiancée, Dolly, chimed in and pleaded for him to leave. Hancock still wouldn't budge, but he did begin to weaken.

"Oh, My Aching Buttocks!"

Samuel Adams didn't learn to ride a horse until September 1775. His younger cousin John Adams finally persuaded Samuel that "skill and dexterity in horsemanship was necessary to the character of a statesman." At first Samuel needed help from two servants. One held the bridle and stirrup, the other boosted the chubby statesman onto the saddle. Eventually John taught Samuel how to lift himself "gracefully onto the seat without the least danger of falling over on the other side." Samuel soon got the hang of it, but after a day of riding, his butt was so sore, he couldn't sit up straight. John told him to buy two yards of flannel to pad his posterior. This, said John, "defended [Samuel] from any further injury."

"If I had my musket," he said, "I would never turn my back upon these troops." But his musket was back in Boston.

Adams took advantage of this slight opening. He walked over, patted Hancock on the shoulder, and reminded him, "[Fighting] is not our business; we belong to the cabinet." He meant the group of men running the Massachusetts Provincial Congress.

Finally, Hancock agreed it would be disastrous for the patriot cause if he or Adams were shot or captured.

Leaving Miss Dolly and Aunt Lydia to finish packing, Hancock, Adams, Lowell, and Revere prepared to depart. Outside, Hancock felt he had to justify his exit to the local security guards: "I wish you to understand that I am not going away because I have any fear. . . . I am not afraid of all the redcoats they can march here. I go at the . . . request of my friend Clarke [who] seems to be alarmed about us, so we go to please him." The men boarded Hancock's coach. The tavern keeper, William Munroe, climbed up into the driver's seat, shook the reins, and drove the patriot leaders toward a safer safe house in Woburn.

The new hideout was about four miles northeast of Lexington, and a good ten miles from Concord. The house was owned by Mrs. Abigail Jones, widow of a deceased Woburn minister. The late Reverend Jones had been an ardent patriot and a trusted friend of Reverend Clarke in Lexington.

Revere, Munroe, and Lowell dropped off Hancock and Adams at the house in Woburn and then returned to Lexington to pick up the ladies, their luggage, and two more things: a trunk and a fish. The trunk was next to Lowell's bed at Buckman Tavern. It was crammed not with Hancock's imported clothes but with reams of revealing and incriminating patriot documents. Not the sort of stuff Hancock wanted to fall into British hands. The fish was a freshwater salmon that a Lexington man had presented to Hancock. Never one to forgo a local delicacy, Hancock planned to have Mrs. Jones sauté it for his breakfast.

While Dolly was wrapping up the salmon, Revere and Lowell hustled toward Buckman Tavern to retrieve the trunk. As they neared the common, a Lexington man named Thaddeus Bowman came galloping up the Great Road, shouting that the regulars were within two miles.

Lexington militia leader John Parker ordered alarm guns fired and summoned a nineteen-year-old apprentice wheelwright named William Diamond. When Diamond wasn't learning how to make or repair wooden wheels, he liked to play the drum, and now Parker ordered Diamond to go out on the common and "beat the drum call to arms." Joining Diamond was Lexington's only fifer, sixteen-year-old Jonathan Harrington, who had taught himself to play the small flute the year before.

Harrington recalled that after his mother woke him around three o'clock in the morning, he dressed quickly, slung a gun over his shoulder, grabbed his fife, and "hurried to the parade near the meeting-house." From there he could see "lights moving" in all ten houses around the common. As men emerged from the houses and others poured out of Buckman Tavern, Harrington said, "I fifed with all my might."

Captain Parker shouted, "Every man of you who is equipped, follow me—and those of you, who are not equipped, go into the meeting house, and furnish yourselves from the [powder] magazine, and immediately join the company."

Now Parker had to decide where to position his men. He could have posted them behind houses, stone walls, and barns, where they could monitor the regulars without provoking them. Instead, he led the company to the northwest end of the common, near the Bedford Road, and ordered them to load their guns.

This command didn't go over so well. One man said, "There are so few of us. It would be folly to stand here." Others agreed.

Parker, like other homegrown military leaders, was usually open to suggestions, but not this time. Upon hearing the grousing, he growled,

"The first man who offers to run shall be shot down." That threat alone may have been enough to hold the men in place. There was also the fact that every fourth man in the line was related to Parker either by blood or by marriage. Whatever each man's reason, nobody ran.

While the militiamen waited for who-knew-what, Revere and Lowell hurried into Buckman Tavern and bounded up the stairs. Hancock's wooden trunk was four feet long, two feet wide, and more than two feet high. Covered with leather, fastened with brass, and packed with papers, it was a major load. The men bent, grimaced, grunted, and raised the thing off the floor. As they moved toward the stairway, Revere glanced out the "chamber window" and saw Major John Pitcairn's 230-man advance column "coming up the road."

Revere and Lowell wrestled the trunk down the narrow stairway and out the door. Continuing across the common, they lurched through the ranks of militiamen, who, according to Revere, now numbered fifty or sixty.

Captain Parker shouted, "Let the troops pass by and don't molest them." Parker apparently thought that if his militiamen just stood there and acted as "an army of observation," nothing violent would happen.

One thing to note here is that Major Pitcairn was *not* at the head of the British advance column. He was halfway to the back. In the front was a fiery young Irishman named Jesse Adair. And now, as the first rays of dawn streaked the sky, Lieutenant Adair also had to make a choice. Should he ignore the rebels on Lexington Common, remain on the Great Road, and continue toward Concord . . . as so ordered? Or should he forget the orders, take the right fork, and confront the impertinent rebels?

A quick word about Adair—he apparently wasn't the brightest bulb on the porch. He was "brave, but brainless," writes Fischer, "quick to act, but sometimes slow to understand." No surprise then that Adair chose to take the right fork. Within minutes, sixty regulars, like two rivers of scarlet, flowed around the meeting house.

A circa 1900 image of a marker commemorating the Lexington Minute Men and their bravery. It is on the Lexington Battle Green (also called Lexington Common) in Lexington, Massachusetts.

Seeing the front half of his advance column swerve to the right, Major Pitcairn galloped toward Lexington Common, where he overtook Lieutenant Adair and rode to within seventy yards of John Parker's patriot militiamen.

"Stand your ground!" Parker shouted to his men.

"Disperse, you damned rebels!" yelled Major Pitcairn.

The rebels did not disperse.

Another British officer, possibly Major Mitchell, yelled, "Lay down your arms!"

No rebel laid down his musket.

Pitcairn screamed, "You dogs, run!"

No rebels ran. Captain Parker may have hoped for a discussion with his British counterpart, but Major Pitcairn wasn't about to negotiate with what he regarded as a ragtag (and treasonous) bunch of rebels.

By this time, Revere and Lowell were clear of the common. That's when the first shots rang out. Revere wrote that he heard a pistol pop, followed by the "continual roar of musketry." With bullets "flying thick about him," Revere dropped the trunk. Lowell followed. They ran behind Jonathan Harrington's house and "into a wood, where [they] halted, and heard the firing for about a quarter of an hour." A British officer said the musket fire "was continued by [British] troops as long as any of the provincials were to be seen."

When the shooting stopped, Revere and Lowell crept out and managed to retrieve the trunk.

And what did Mr. Longfellow say about this harrowing scene?

A drawing of the Battle of Lexington, artist and date unknown.

Chapter 9

First Blood

Sorry again, I agree it's absurd
That Longfellow skimped on what had occurred.

The poet gave us no description nor any details of the skirmish in Lexington. All we got from him is a measly two words: "bloody work." Well, he was right about that.

Who started the shooting on Lexington Common? Historians aren't sure. Eyewitness accounts vary. Revere wrote that after the pistol pop, he "saw the smoke in front of the troops." He said the front line of regulars "gave a great shout, ran a few paces and then the whole [line] fired."

Fifer Jonathan Harrington said it was "the angry leader of the regulars" who "fired his pistol and ordered his men to shoot." When some of the British soldiers fired over the heads of the patriots, Major Pitcairn reportedly shouted, "God damn you, fire *at* them!" But he later denied that. In his report to General Gage, Pitcairn said the first shots were fired not by him, not by his soldiers, and not by any of Parker's militiamen, but rather by some trigger-happy locals on the periphery of the common. From behind a stone wall, these Lexington rebels "fired four or five shots at the soldiers" and wounded Pitcairn's horse and one of the regulars. Only at that point, Pitcairn wrote, did his light infantry "begin a scattered fire."

Changing Perspectives

The uncertainty of what happened at Lexington is reflected in many prints, sketches, engravings, lithographs, and paintings. A 1775 print made by Amos Doolittle shows no colonists firing. Such nonviolence on the patriot side is exactly what Dr. Warren and Samuel Adams wanted all the colonies, and the rest of the world, to see.

Over the next fifty years, as the glory of the Revolution grew, and as Lexington and Concord engaged in competition over where the war started, painters portrayed the Lexington men less as victims and more as combatants. An 1830 William S. Pendleton lithograph shows eight militiamen standing their ground. Two are loading their guns, and six are shooting. An 1855 Hammatt Billings engraving increases the number of Lexington men firing to about twelve. And in *Dawn of Liberty*, an 1886 Henry Sandham painting, John Parker's line holds, and no militiamen disperse. The town of Lexington paid Sandham four thousand dollars for that painting, and like the Longfellow poem, it is a willful distortion of history. It still hangs in Lexington Town Hall.

With each side eager to accuse the other of firing first, the true instigator will likely never be known. But the aftermath was brutally clear. Eight patriots lay dead, nine more were bleeding from bullet and bayonet wounds, and rampaging regulars were chasing after retreating rebels.

At this point, the British commander, Colonel Smith, finally caught up with Major Pitcairn. Riding onto Lexington Common, Smith was shocked by the chaos and the carnage. This was not part of the plan. Lexington should have been bypassed. Pitcairn should not have blood on his hands. And the British advance column should be hotfooting it toward the two bridges in Concord. In his report Colonel Smith wrote that he was "desirous of putting a stop to all further slaughter of these deluded people," so he ordered the drumbeat to call back the regulars from their rebel hunt.

"We then formed on the Common," wrote one British officer, "but with some difficulty, the men were so wild they could hear no orders."

To restore decorum, Colonel Smith called for "three hazzas" and a victory volley, whereupon eight hundred British muskets delivered a booming aftershock to the already traumatized citizens of Lexington.

Smith summoned his junior officers. Up to this moment, to ensure secrecy, these officers had not been told where they were headed or why. Only now, as they stood on blood-soaked Lexington Common, did Colonel Smith reveal that they were marching to Concord, "to destroy a magazine of stores collected there."

The officers were well aware that questioning an order was risky and could end their careers. Still, some of them bravely spoke up. With the countryside "being alarmed and [rebels] assembling," they said, it would be "impracticable" to advance to Concord. They "advised Col Smith to give up the idea of prosecuting his march and to return to Boston." But Smith had been a military man for nearly three decades. Retirement was near. To his credit, Smith "listened politely" and issued no reprimands. Then he said he was "determined to obey the orders he had received."

A postcard of the 1886 mural The Dawn of Liberty *by Henry Sandham. The mural is in Cary Memorial Hall, Lexington, Massachusetts.*

Smith told his soldiers to refill their cartridge boxes with ammunition and sent teams of regulars to take positions one hundred yards north and south of the main column. These flankers would flush out any rebel snipers lurking in the fields, swamps, and woodlands. Officers shouted commands, and the eight hundred red-coated regulars moved westward.

Meanwhile, Revere and Lowell had made it back to the Clarke house, where they hoisted Hancock's trunk onto the yellow coach. Revere went in to fetch Aunt Lydia, who was weeping, and Miss Dolly, who was helping Reverend Clarke hide money and watches among the potatoes. The ladies said their goodbyes, and Lowell helped them into the coach. Revere climbed into the driver's perch and snapped the reins, and they headed north.

Reaching Mrs. Jones's house in Woburn, Revere could give Hancock and Adams only a vague account of the fight, because a house (and gun smoke) had reduced his view. Aunt Lydia spoke of peeking out the Clarke house's door only to have a bullet whiz by her head and strike the barn. Miss Dolly said that after the shootout, two men were brought to the Clarke house. She reported that "one of them, whose head was grazed by a ball, insisted on it that he was dead; the other, who was shot in the arm, behaved better."

Ready, Aim, Phew!

A thirty-five-year-old farmer named Joshua Simonds was in charge of Lexington's gunpowder, which was stored in one of the upper galleries of the meeting house. Simonds was filling three militiamen's powder horns when the regulars rushed onto the common. Two of the militiamen ran outside and were shot. The third looked out the window and shouted, "We are . . . surrounded!" He hid in the opposite gallery. Simonds stayed put. When the shooting stopped, a British officer shouted, "Clear that house!" Simonds heard footsteps on the stairs. He decided that if he had to die, he would not go quietly. He cocked his gun and placed the muzzle inches from an open cask of gunpowder. The footsteps come closer . . . Simonds waited . . . closed his eyes . . . and . . . then out on Lexington Common, a British drummer pounded out a message: cease hostilities. The footsteps came no closer, and Simonds lived another thirty years.

Mrs. Jones pan-fried and served Hancock's freshwater salmon. But before anyone could take a bite, "a messenger from Lexington rushed in," gave a grisly description of the bloodshed there, and warned the patriot leaders that they were being "hotly pursued." Hancock ordered his enslaved man Cuff to drive the conspicuous yellow coach into the woods and conceal it. Convinced that the women would not be harmed, Hancock, Adams, and Revere squeezed into Mrs. Jones's coach, and a local man "piloted" them "by a cart-way" three miles to Amos Wyman's house "in an obscure corner of Bedford, Burlington and Billerica."

Missing his fresh salmon and by now very hungry, Hancock pretended to enjoy Mrs. Wyman's humble offering of cold salt pork, brown bread, and potatoes. Later he sent the Wymans' daughter a thank-you gift: a cow.

Revere was probably still with Hancock and Adams for that modest meal. Where he went from the Wyman house, no one can say.

But here are two things we *can* say: The Revolutionary War began on the morning of April 19, 1775, on the common in Lexington. And only in Longfellow's imagination did Paul Revere ever ride into Concord town.

The Lexington Minute Men, ***by Bashka Paeff, was installed in 1948 near Lexington Green and Buckman Tavern. Along the bottom it says, "These men gave everything in life yea and life itself in support of the common cause."***

The Minute Man *statue in Minute Man National Park in Concord, Massachusetts, was created by Daniel Chester French and was unveiled on April 19, 1875, the 100th anniversary of the battle. The statue is seven feet tall and was made from Civil War cannons. There are two time capsules in the base: one placed in 1875 and one placed in 1975.*

Chapter 10

"For God's Sake, Fire!"

And one was safe and asleep in his bed
Who at the bridge would be first to fall,
Who that day would be lying dead,
Pierced by a British musket-ball.

Longfellow never saw a movie. He missed the first one by just fourteen years. Nevertheless, "Paul Revere's Ride" has a scene-shifting, cinematic quality. Earlier we noted Longfellow's "decisive cut" from the North Church to the Charlestown shore. Now he made another such cut as he pivoted from Revere to a new, secondary character who was supposedly sound asleep despite the gunshots and clanging bells.

The poet didn't name this doomed fellow, but the history books (which Longfellow had certainly read) say that the first to fall at the North Bridge in Concord was Isaac Davis, a thirty-year-old captain of the Acton minutemen. This raises some questions. How did an Acton man wind up at the front of the patriot column? Shouldn't Concord men have been in the lead? And why did fighting break out a mile outside town? Why not on Concord Common in the center of town?

To help find the answers, let's utilize our own decisive cut and vault ahead to mid-morning on April 19, 1775. Imagine you were there in

Long Night

Isaac Davis had four children under the age of ten. All were sick on April 19, so it's unlikely he was "asleep in his bed," as Longfellow wrote.

Concord: clear skies, light wind from the west, not quite fifty degrees, nine o'clock in the morning.

The regulars (having marched into Concord around seven thirty in the morning) were arrayed as follows: Four hundred and fifty soldiers searched for military stores in the town center. One hundred more held the South Bridge and searched houses on both sides of the bridge. Another 150 regulars under Captain Lawrence Parsons poked around James Barrett's house and barn, and a hundred under Captain Walter Laurie held the North Bridge.

As for the patriots, James Barrett had concluded that morning that he didn't have nearly enough fighters to confront the eight hundred regulars. So Barrett had led his two hundred Concord men on a retreat northward to a flat-topped hill just west of John Buttrick's place. There, not only did they have a good view of the hundred regulars at the North Bridge, but they could also signal to patriots arriving from nearby towns. And, boy, did they arrive—seventy-seven from Bedford, sixty-two from Lincoln, ninety or so from Acton, sixteen from Carlisle and Billerica, nine from Groton, four from Westford, "several squads of men from Littleton, Chelmsford . . . and Stow," and Reverend Brooks from Medford, the first town that Paul Revere had alarmed. By nine thirty that morning, Barrett had close to five hundred patriots under arms, and Paul Revere's late-night bluff to Major Mitchell had become a reality. A British officer at the North Bridge called Barrett's army "a formidable force."

At the same time, the regulars on Main Street began burning the few military stores they found—some wooden gun carriages and a heap of wooden spoons and cutting boards. A spark from the blaze jumped to

the courthouse, and soon that building burned, too. In a weird moment of unity, a few of the older townspeople and a line of regulars formed a bucket brigade to douse the flames, but by that time a plume of smoke had risen high into the sky. Barrett's patriots up on the training field couldn't see what was on fire, but some feared it was their houses.

Barrett huddled with John Buttrick and patriot commanders from other towns. A minute went by, then another. Joseph Hosmer, the thirty-nine-year-old cabinet maker, stepped onto a stump and shouted, "I have . . . heard . . . the British boast that they could march through our country, laying waste our hamlets and villages and we would not oppose them. And *I begin to think it is true*." He pointed to the smoke, turned to Barrett, and shouted, "Will you let them burn down the town?"

In no professional army would a lowly lieutenant dare to speak out that way. But this was the New England militia, where the democratic spirit of the town meeting carried over onto the battlefield.

Many of the assembled patriots agreed with Hosmer that something must be done. As the gung-ho spirit burbled and built, Captain William Smith of Lincoln announced that he and his men were ready to "dislodge" regulars from the bridge. But Barrett and the other commanders wouldn't be rushed, and their huddle continued.

Some minuteman mythology portrays these farmers, gunsmiths, chair

"Where's Your Bucket?"

Had the regulars not started a fire in the center of Concord, the patriots might not have marched on the North Bridge. In colonial towns, fire was a constant threat, and whenever a blaze broke out, all able-bodied citizens helped. While there was no official fire department in Concord until 1794, every adult male had two leather buckets with his name on them. Old, sick, and disabled citizens unable to fight a fire were still expected to toss their buckets outside so someone could take them along. A fire warden was appointed, and he would stay on site after a fire had been extinguished and note the names on the buckets. Any man whose bucket was missing was fined.

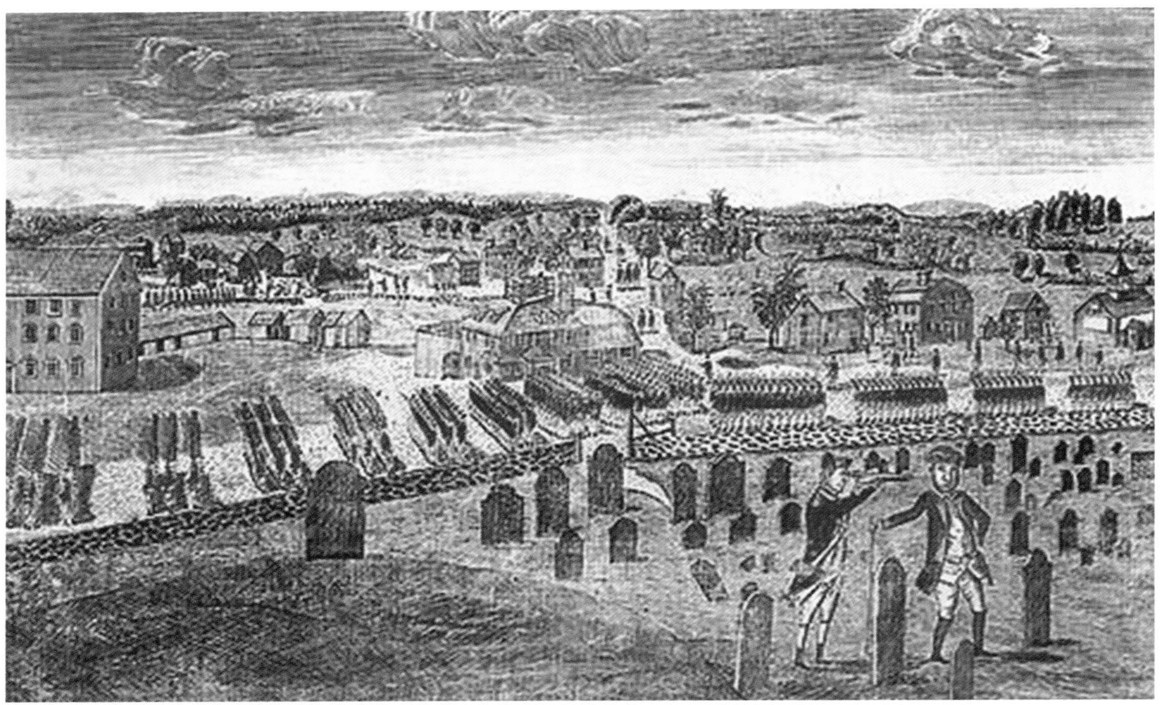

A photograph of an engraving by Amos Doolittle of the British troops marching through Concord.

makers, chandlers, and coopers in their floppy hats and brown homespun clothing as military amateurs. The truth is, they weren't spur-of-the-moment soldiers, and this was no amateur hour. All winter, these men drilled eight times a month, in drafty barns, on frozen fields, and in the case of the minutemen from Reading, "in the large kitchen of the parsonage." In Acton, Isaac Davis built a firing range behind his gun shop, and starting in November 1774, his men took target practice twice a week. In Woburn, the town council voted to pay minutemen to "inform themselves in the science of handling their firelocks," and fines were levied for any "non appearance" at the muster. And in Concord, the town voted in January 1775 to appoint a muster master, to provide a drum for the minutemen, to raise the pay of company captains, to lend muskets to the fifteen men who lacked a firearm, to furnish one hundred minutemen

with ammunition boxes, and to hire a "master in gunnery" to teach forty locals how to fire a cannon.

Certainly most, if not all, of these patriots were prepared for a confrontation. One question remained: Would they be given the order to advance . . . and fire?

It was nearly ten o'clock when James Barrett broke away from the huddle and announced that a unanimous decision had been reached. We will "march into the middle of the town to defend our homes, or die in the attempt." Barrett ordered the men to load their guns. "Many had done so already; some deliberately double-shotted their muskets."

Before they marched, Barrett rode along the line and gave strict orders not to fire first. Four hours earlier, Captain Parker had given the same order in Lexington. This was no accident.

The script for Colonial resistance was well known, having been disseminated by political leaders, field commanders, and clergy. Concord reverend William Emerson summed it up in a March 1775 sermon: "Let every single step taken in this most intricate affair be upon the defensive. God forbid that we should give our enemies the opportunity of saying justly that we have brought a civil war upon ourselves, by the smallest offensive action."

As the Concord companies took their places at the head of the muster, John Buttrick suddenly realized there was a problem. Those men had no bayonets. What would happen, he wondered, if instead of firing at the patriots, the regulars guarding the west end of the North Bridge presented their bayonets and threatened to skewer any Concord man who tried to cross? What then?

Buttrick hurried down the line to consult with Acton's Isaac Davis, who, in his gun shop, had forged bayonets for every one of his minutemen. As a result, they were the only company on the hill equipped for hand-to-hand combat. Davis assured Buttrick that he and his men were

ready to take the lead, which they did. And that's how the Acton men wound up in front.

The patriots moved off the hill in double file. A British officer at the bridge reported that the rebels marched "with a[s] much order as the best disciplined troops."

Historian Allen French writes that on April 19, Colonel James Barrett was "unable to march." The sixty-five-year-old farmer likely had bad knees. So forty-three-year-old John Buttrick took command. Barrett remained atop his horse and "rode nearer the rear [of the column] where he could exert his influence over the [many] militia companies." A group of boys, including Barrett's eleven-year-old grandson, Nathan, tagged along behind Barrett's horse. These kids often mimicked their dads and granddads during training exercises.

Cider Man

Concord's Reverend William Emerson reported that an hour before the shoot-out at the North Bridge, a "crazy man" was wandering around with two jugs of hard cider, offering drinks both to patriots on the hillside and regulars at the bridge. His name was Elias Brown, and he was so feebleminded that his family and friends thought him "incapable of managing any business." Well, on the morning of April 19, he did a fine job of quenching the thirst of fighters on both sides. For a sliver of time, Brown "may have been the sanest person in town."

Coming off the hill, the patriots curled to the left and continued down the sinuous causeway by the Concord River. Ahead they could see the regulars prying the wooden planks off the North Bridge, the very planks that John Buttrick had pounded into place not long before. Such destruction would soon render the bridge impassable.

When Buttrick got about a hundred yards from the bridge, he hollered at the regulars to stop tearing up the planks. The regulars "desisted and formed for action." Buttrick called a halt, turned to his men, and said that if they all agreed, they would charge and "drive them away from the

bridge." The minutemen talked briefly, then all agreed. Buttrick gave a shout, and the men ran toward the bridge.

The regulars fired three warning shots that flew high and plunked into the Concord River. "Their balls whistled well," said patriot Amos Barrett, but they didn't slow the onrushing patriots. A fourth ball wounded the Acton fifer, Luther Blanchard, but still the patriots pressed on. Fifty yards, forty, and then, on the British side, "a general popping . . . ensued" as two companies of regulars "gave afire."

A marble-sized ball slammed into Isaac Davis's chest, lifted him off his feet, and flung him backward. "His blood gushed out in one great stream, flying, it is said, more than ten feet, besprinkling and besmearing . . . the clothes" of the two Acton men nearest him. Even in death, Davis clutched his gun so tightly it had to be pried from his hand.

Some patriots were luckier: Joshua Brooks of Lincoln had a ball pass through his hat. So did Acton's Ezekiel Davis, a brother of the captain. Abner Hosmer, another Acton man, was not so lucky. He took a ball in the forehead and fell dead.

Colonel Barrett's orders not to fire first were so strictly observed that the patriots received the fire of the enemy in three separate discharges before Buttrick finally roared, "Fire, fellow soldiers, for God's sake fire!"

Buttrick steadied himself and "fired his own piece," and so did every patriot with a clear shot. With the balls flying, Barrett's grandson and his preteen posse turned around and sprinted the other way.

The initial patriot blast killed two British infantrymen, wounded several others, and bloodied four of the eight British officers. One of them, Lieutenant Sutherland, wrote that he "received a shot a little above my right breast which turned me half round."

Even before the patriots could reload their guns, the British line broke, and the regulars fled "like a flock of sheep." One Concord fighter remembered, "It was not more than two minutes, if so much, till

Battle at Concord Bridge: reenactment, *made by photographer Leslie Jones in 1928 at Minute Man National Park on the Old North Bridge. Reenactments of the famous battle happen every April.*

the British run and the fire ceased." Another patriot reported, "There was eight or ten that were wounded and a running and a hobbling about looking back to see if we was after them."

For the patriots, it was a stunning result. So stunning, in fact, that the Massachusetts men halted their pursuit just east of the bridge. There they simply stood and stared at a sight they'd never seen before: regulars running for their lives. Most patriots forgot all about Colonel Barrett's order to march into the center of Concord. Formations and discipline broke down as no one seemed to know what to do next. Major Buttrick managed to round up the scattered Concord and Acton men and deploy them behind a stone wall "back of Elisha Jones's house." There they

waited for a possible British counterattack. Other patriots retreated. A few even left for home. Minuteman Thaddeus Blood said, "After the fire everyone appeared to be his own commander."

Several men carried the bodies of Isaac Davis and Abner Hosmer to Buttrick's hillside house. Colonel Barrett sent other wounded patriots to his house. At Reverend Emerson's house, women and children gathered, seeking safety and spiritual guidance.

When it became apparent there would be no British counterattack, the patriot fighters sat down under trees, drank from their canteens, and ate whatever snacks they had stuffed into their pockets. The four men from Westford had left home too quickly to pack snacks, but luckily for them, a fourteen-year-old lad had followed them to Concord, carrying "a bushel of doughnuts."

In the center of Concord, British army surgeons bandaged the wounded regulars who could still walk. Soldiers unable to walk were lifted into horse-drawn carriages padded with bedding, pillows, and women's apparel, all stolen from nearby houses.

Colonel Smith climbed the hill behind Brown's house, elongated his spyglass, and peered toward the North Bridge. He saw Captain Lawrence Parsons and his 120 regulars returning from their unsuccessful search-and-destroy mission at James Barrett's farm, and Colonel Smith wasn't sure what would happen when those regulars reached the North Bridge. What if the rebels opened fire? As Captain Parsons's men neared the bridge, the picnicking patriots dropped their snack packs and gripped their muskets. With Parson's detachment mightily outnumbered, the patriots could easily have inflicted heavy casualties or made prisoners of the regulars. The Massachusetts men awaited their orders. But both James Barrett and John Buttrick stayed silent.

This irked Acton minuteman Solomon Smith, who later testified, "It was owing to our want of order and our confused state that [Parsons's

regulars] were not taken prisoners." Another Acton man, Thomas Thorp, complained that no one "assumed any command." It may have been disorder, it may have been James Barrett's Hamlet moment ("to fire or not to fire"), or it may have been Barrett and Buttrick's deep-rooted reluctance "to attack the king's troops without cause." Captain Parsons certainly gave them no cause. In fact, after seeing the hundreds of armed rebels lining the road, Parsons and his men were so eager to get across the North Bridge and back to Concord Common that they didn't even stop to pick up their two dead comrades, who had the dubious distinction of being "the first British combat deaths in the Revolutionary War." As soon as Parsons's regulars came into view, Colonel Smith turned his spyglass eastward. Hoping to catch a glimpse of red-coated reinforcements, all he saw was an empty roadway. He had no way of knowing that his early-morning request for reinforcements had been mishandled, and the orders to assemble the Royal Marines were mistakenly sent to Major John Pitcairn's empty apartment. As a result, General Hugh Percy's relief force did not leave Boston until after nine in the morning. Finally, at noon, Colonel Smith concluded that he could wait no longer. He climbed onto his horse and "ordered his men . . . into marching formation." Flankers assigned to protect the column headed for the ridgeline north of the road and into the pasture land to the south. The long column moved out.

Concord minuteman Amos Barrett recalled, "We found them a marching back towards Boston [and] we was soon after them." While some patriots hung on the rear of the British column, others ran eastward through Elisha Jones's pasture and took concealed positions on both sides of the Great Road.

These patriots were soon joined by 270 fighters from Reading. One of the Reading men was a volunteer named Edmund Foster. He was a Yale University divinity student who happened to be home on spring break.

On April 19, "just at sunrise, *alarm guns* were fired, which were quickly followed by [an express] bringing news, that the regulars . . . had gone to Concord." Foster hopped out of bed, dressed, ran to the nearby home of a minuteman commander, and asked if he was "going to *Concord* and *when*. Immediately, was the answer." Foster said he "borrowed accoutrements" and marched the sixteen miles from Reading to Concord. Behind a barn near Meriam's Corner, Foster watched the long column of redcoats come into view. There was no fifing, no drumming, no shouted commands; only the measured tread of weary soldiers and "the mournful creak of the ambulance carriages." Foster recalled that "silence reigned on both sides."

The regulars approached the narrow bridge over Elm Brook. If the British flankers continued north and south of the column, they would have to wade through the icy water.

Instead, they angled down toward the road and merged with the main column. With no flanker-fear the patriots closed in. As the first regulars tramped over the bridge, a Reading man fired—and missed. The regulars faced about, "presented muskets," and fired back. Their balls flew high. A British officer later admitted, "This ineffectual fire gave the rebels more confidence, as they soon found . . . they suffered but little from it." The Reading men pushed forward and "returned fire with greater accuracy." Two British infantrymen fell dead near the brook, while an officer, Ensign Jeremy Lister, took a bullet in the right elbow joint, "the ball," he wrote, "having gone through the bone and lodged within the skin."

Now the Great Road turned into a battle road.

And Longfellow took us right into the midst of the ferocious, ball-for-ball combat.

This engraving of the Battle of Lexington was originally published in A Brief History of the United States *in 1885. Artist unknown.*

Chapter 11

Battle Road

You know the rest. In the books you have read,
How the British Regulars fired and fled,—
How the farmers gave them ball for ball,
From behind each fence and farm-yard wall,
Chasing the red-coats down the lane,
Then crossing the fields to emerge again
Under the trees at the turn of the road,
And only pausing to fire and load.

Ensign Lister wrote, “It . . . became a general firing upon us from all quarters, from behind hedges and walls.” Another British officer wrote, “They were so concealed there was hardly any seeing them.”

As the regulars slogged eastward, the patriot army was augmented by 237 men from Sudbury, 149 from Framingham, 104 from Chelmsford, 101 from Billerica, and 33 from Tewksbury. Eager to keep his young fighters hidden behind the sheltering trees, Tewksbury’s minuteman commander, John Trull, shouted, “Stand trim, men, or the rascals will shoot your elbows off.”

By the time the regulars reached the Concord-Lincoln town line, the “landscape was alive with armed men . . . the hills echoed and flashed,

Fast Food

In Lincoln, as soon as the column of regulars straggled through town, some women went outside. Knowing that their husbands and sons would be right behind, they laid boards across two barrels and put out a picnic lunch of "hasty pudding and milk."

the woods rang, and the road became an endless ambuscade of flame."

One British officer wrote, "The rebels were monstrous, numerous and surrounded us on every side." Another officer noted that "the fire . . . never slackened." A third wrote, "I had my hat shot off my head three times, [and] two balls went through my coat and carried away my bayonet."

Look again at the introduction to this battle stanza. "You know the rest. In the books you have read." This is a neat trick. Longfellow, in essence, put his arm around the reader and said, "Help me finish the story."

Professor Gioia says, "Ingeniously, Longfellow acknowledges the importance of the . . . battle without accepting the artistic necessity to describe it in detail."

Just in case you're a little foggy on what Longfellow meant by "the rest," you should know that the battle raged for seven hours, and the battlefield extended for seventeen miles, all the way from the eastern edge of Concord to the Charlestown peninsula. During the fighting, the British suffered around 270 casualties (that is, killed, wounded, or missing), the patriots just 94. It was not until midnight that the last of the fleeing regulars were ferried across the Charles River to Boston.

When the wounded and wobbly Jeremy Lister arrived at his lodging, he asked his landlady for "a dish of tea." In the prior twenty-four hours, he had marched forty miles, been blasted in the elbow, lost a lot of blood, and eaten nothing but a bite of biscuit and beef. "It is beyond the power of words," he wrote, "to express the satisfaction I felt from that tea."

In his official report, General Gage admitted that the Concord mission had been undermined by a well-designed colonial alarm system.

In his stirring summation, Longfellow celebrated Revere as the point man of this far-reaching network.

So through the night rode Paul Revere
And so through the night went his cry of alarm
To every Middlesex village and farm,—
A cry of defiance and not of fear,
A voice in the darkness, a knock at the door,
And a word that shall echo forevermore!

Gioia says that in this stanza, Longfellow transformed Revere from an actual historical figure to a "timeless emblem of American courage and independence." One tip-off for this transformation is the change in tense. Longfellow went from past tense "rode" and "went" to future tense "shall echo" and, in the following lines, "will waken."

For, borne on the night-wind of the Past,
Through all our history, to the last,
In the hour of darkness and peril and need,
The people will waken and listen to hear
The hurrying hoof-beats of that steed,
And the midnight message of Paul Revere.

On the night of April 18, 1775, Revere's voice in the darkness shouted, "The regulars are coming!" The next night, that same voice was likely asking for a bed and a pillow.

One Tough Cookie

Hearing that the retreating regulars were near, seventy-eight-year-old Menotomy man Samuel Whittemore told his wife he was joining the fight. Armed with a musket, a sword, and a pair of pistols, Whittemore found a position behind a stone wall near Cooper's Tavern. Whittemore aimed his musket and shot one soldier in the chest. A pistol shot killed another, and a second pistol shot bloodied a third, who later died. Whittemore was then shot in the face, beaten by muskets, and stabbed thirteen times. Later, one of the soldiers said, "We killed an old devil in Menotomy, but we paid almost too dear for it."

It turned out the soldier was only half right. Whittemore's blood-soaked body was carted to Cooper's Tavern. Dr. Cotton Tufts of Medford took one look, cupped Whittemore's wrist, and was about to pronounce him dead, but there was a faint pulse! Still, what chance did the old man have? Tufts tended to other patients, and eventually he and two other surgeons dressed Whittemore's cheek and his stab wounds. Wouldn't you know, that old geezer lived for another eighteen years!

Where Revere slept on April 19 he never mentioned in his writing. It was probably somewhere close to Boston, because on the morning of April 20, he was in Cambridge, meeting with Dr. Warren's Committee of Safety. At this volatile and unprecedented moment, the parlor of Jonathan Hastings's house, near the Harvard University campus, was serving as the colony's temporary seat of government, and Warren's committee became the closest thing Massachusetts had to a governing authority. During a break in the proceedings, Revere wrote a letter to his wife, Rachel, asking her to bring him just what anyone would want after thirty-six hours on the road: clean socks and underwear.

On that same day, Revere noted that Dr. Warren "engaged me as a messenger to do the out of doors business" for the Committee of Safety. Revere spent the next seventeen days in the saddle, carrying to towns and villages Dr. Warren's letter, which implored men to enlist in the patriot army "to defend our wives and children from the butchering hands of the inhuman soldiery." For these rides

Revere charged the committee five shillings a day, plus "expenses for self and horse."

As for the midnight ride, Revere asked for no payment. Eventually, of course, he would be rewarded for that ride with the gift of immortality.

Which brings us back to Mr. Longfellow and his poetic version of history.

This drawing represents the desire to free Black people from slavery. Broken shackles fall from a basket lifted by an eagle holding two American flags with the words "All men are created equal. Stand by the declaration." A Black man and a white man sit together and "Break every yoke; let the oppressed go free" is written above them. Created by artist Dominique C. Fabronius with lithographer L. Prang & Co., it was published by B. W. Thayer & Co. in Boston in 1861, just before the Civil War.

Chapter 12

American Mythology

The poem having ended, the moment is nigh to answer the question: Why did Longfellow lie?

In order to confer immortality on a mere mortal and to make Revere's ride one that "shall echo forevermore," Longfellow had to make some big changes. He pushed aside the real Revere (and the real midnight ride) to create a mythical Revere—a solitary hero who rowed alone across a river, who rode alone across the countryside, and who galloped alone into Concord, shouting a cry of defiance, not fear.

This great-man version of the midnight ride required Longfellow to eliminate all but one of Revere's compatriots. Historian Harold Murdock complains that "in glorifying Paul Revere . . . Longfellow innocently robbed William Dawes and Dr. Prescott of well-earned honors." Simplifying the story allowed the poet to craft a more concise and compelling narrative. It also allowed him to embed an urgent political message in the poem.

Recall that Longfellow began writing "Paul Revere's Ride" in April 1860. At that time, it seemed that the United States would break apart over the issue of slavery. In every state, people talked about the possibility of civil war. On one side were men and women known as abolitionists. They wanted the United States government to abolish slavery,

a practice they knew was cruel and immoral. On the other side were Southern plantation owners whose wealth and power would shrivel if they had no enslaved people to plant and harvest the rice, tobacco, indigo, and cotton on which their fortunes were built. These plantation owners and their elected representatives in Washington, DC, told the abolitionists to mind their own business, and to heed "the great truth that the Negro is not equal to the white man" and "slavery is his natural and normal condition." Southern lawmakers threatened that South Carolina, Mississippi, Florida, Alabama, Georgia, Louisiana, and five other Southern states would secede from the United States and form their own confederacy if the federal government dared to abolish slavery.

Newly elected president Abraham Lincoln told voters, "I have always hated slavery, I think as much as any abolitionist." But Lincoln also feared a fractured country. Hoping to save the Union, he initially assured slave owners that he would not ban slavery in states where it already existed. He thought there could be a compromise to ban it in the new Western territories, where he said there should be "free labor on free soil."

When Longfellow read that, he was horrified. He liked the new president, but he thought this trade-off was a terrible idea. When it came to slavery, Longfellow saw no room for compromise or concession. "Compromise [is] only a euphemism for surrender," he wrote. Longfellow wanted the president to stand firm and end the buying and selling of human beings in the Southern states and everywhere else in the nation.

This was not a new position for Longfellow. In 1842, he had published *Poems on Slavery*, all eight of which lamented the woes of bondage. One poem called for "this land" to revoke the "whips and yokes" that "insult humanity." In response to a critic, he wrote that slavery was an "unrighteous institution based on the false maxim that might makes right." Longfellow was not what you'd call an active abolitionist. He made no antislavery speeches, like his friends did. He hid no people fleeing slavery in

his cellar, like his friends did. And he never rebuked wealthy Bostonians (like his father-in-law, Nathan Appleton) who bought Southern cotton for their mills and defended plantation owners.

> ### One of a Kind
>
> Big-time portrait painter John Singleton Copley usually painted men wearing wigs and waistcoats. His painting of Paul Revere is Copley's only finished portrait of an artisan dressed in shirt-sleeves and shown working. According to art historian Hermann Williams Jr., it took "a man of independent character like Paul Revere to choose to be painted plying his craft." You can find a photo of the painting on page xvi of this book.

But during the 1850s, Longfellow's journal entries are full of rage about the presence of so-called slave hunters in Boston. In his letters he praised a longtime friend, Massachusetts senator Charles Sumner, for fearlessly denouncing slavery and slaveholders. And in his account books, he recorded the hundreds of dollars he sent to people fleeing slavery, prominent abolitionists, and various anti-slavery societies. Longfellow's son Ernest described his father as more "placid stream than rushing river," but obviously plenty of egalitarian passion bubbled beneath that surface.

It was May 1856, in Washington, DC, when Senator Sumner stood on the Senate floor and reminded his colleagues that slavery was "a crime against nature from which the soul recoils." What Sumner might have added was that the crime was first committed in the American colonies way back in 1619. That's when a warship dropped anchor at Hampton, Virginia, and off-loaded twenty captured Africans who were put to work in the tobacco fields.

Nearly 170 years later, in the spring and summer of 1787, George Washington, Benjamin Franklin, Alexander Hamilton, James Madison, and fifty-one other delegates met in Philadelphia, where they spent five months crafting a Constitution for the thirteen states. After hammering out details for the legislative, executive, and judicial branches, they turned to

Team Effort

On October 13, 1860, Longfellow wrote "Finished" on the bottom of the last page of "Paul Revere's Ride."

Sometime during the first week of November, *Atlantic Monthly* publisher James Fields paid fifty dollars for the rights to print the poem. He called "Paul Revere's Ride" a "fine piece of poetry and painting."

On November 23, Fields urged Longfellow to change the ending. Longfellow had written this:

In the hour of peril men will hear
The midnight message of Paul Revere,
And the hurrying hoof-beat of his steed.

Fields suggested this:

In the hour of darkness and peril and need,
The People will waken and listen to hear
The hurrying hoof-beat of his steed
And the midnight message of Paul Revere.

Fields wrote, "It seems to me the last line as it stands above is stronger. What do you say?" Longfellow agreed and made a few tweaks. He changed the uppercase *P* in "People" to lowercase, made "hoof-beat" plural, and changed "his steed" to "that steed."

the issue of slavery. While some of the Northern delegates called the slave trade "iniquitous" and "nefarious," South Carolina plantation owner Charles Pinckney warned that his state would "not agree to any government which prohibited the slave trade." Abraham Baldwin of Georgia said that laws governing slavery should be left up to the individual states. After much heated debate, a three-point compromise was reached. Point one: when adding up a state's population, for the purpose of representation, an enslaved person would count as three-fifths of a free person. Point two: any enslaved man or woman who escaped from one state and was captured in another state had to be returned to his or her owner. Point three: the slave trade must end in 1808. The slave *trade*, that is. But not slavery itself. That meant that all enslaved people who were already in the United States would stay in bondage, as would any child born to an enslaved woman.

Meanwhile, across the Atlantic Ocean, England abolished slavery in 1807, Spain in 1811, and France in 1848. Ten years later, in February 1858, Senator Sumner urged his pal

Longfellow to lend his talents to the fight for abolition. Referring to Longfellow's 1842 *Poems on Slavery*, Sumner wrote, "I long for another anti-slavery poem from you."

Longfellow replied, "I groan with you over the iniquity of the times . . . and I long to say some vibrant word that should have vitality in it, and force. Be sure if it comes to me I will not be slow in uttering it."

Senator Sumner and his fellow abolitionists waited two more years, but finally, in April 1860, vibrant and vital words flowed from Longfellow's pencil. Like all great poets, he came at his subject poetically.

Longfellow didn't harp on the sorry state of current affairs. He didn't even mention slavery or the impending civil war. Instead, he took his readers back eighty-five years and reminded them about courage. He pointed to a humble silversmith and the embattled farmers at the North Bridge. With his country facing another hour of darkness, peril, and need, Longfellow celebrated the defiant patriots of 1775. In effect, he challenged Americans in 1861 to live up to their country's heroic tradition.

Not All There

Eager to boost magazine sales, Fields slipped the poem to the *Boston Evening Transcript*. On December 18, 1860, "Paul Revere's Ride" was published in the upper-left corner of the front page, surrounded by advertisements for sewing machines, Steinway pianos, and "an entirely new" South American remedy for piles (hemorrhoids).

There was only one problem. The six lines of the poem about Revere's gallop along the Mystic River were left out. Longfellow had accidentally omitted them when he copied the poem for Fields. The *Atlantic* had already gone to press, so it also lacked those six lines when it appeared on newsstands on December 20. A complete version of the poem did not appear until the 1863 publication of *Tales of a Wayside Inn*.

We know from history books that one person can inspire millions; one person can change the course of events. But can a poem do that? Admittedly it's hard to quantify the impact of any work of art. But given

Longfellow's popularity, and given his ability, as Professor Gioia says, "to shape the way nineteenth-century Americans saw themselves, their nation, and their past," it's safe to assume that when "Paul Revere's Ride" was first published in December 1860, it amplified the voices of those determined to preserve the nation and to end the scourge of slavery.

Historian Fischer concurs. He says the poem's galloping rhythm "reverberated through the North like a drum roll," and the poem reinforced the idea that "one man alone could make a difference by his service to a great and noble cause."

According to Professor Angela Sorby, early readers of the poem understood that "Paul Revere's Ride" was a Civil War poem "invoking the founding fathers to support the Union cause." Longfellow's friend Francis Underwood wrote in 1882 that "it cannot have been a mere coincidence that this thrilling poem should have been [published] three months before the outbreak of our Civil War." He went on to say that it was "written to have an influence on the public mind in regard to slavery and the impending war." A 1913 guide for public school teachers emphasized this point, noting that students couldn't appreciate "Paul Revere's Ride" unless they understood the connection between Revere's warning and Longfellow's wake-up call. Teachers no doubt made the point that both men were conveying variations of the same message: namely, that freedom and justice for all are precious and worth fighting for.

Over time, though, old teachers' guides went out of print, and most everyone lost sight of Longfellow's original motive for writing his poem. But it's precisely his motive that explains Longfellow's indifference to the facts. He didn't write the poem to inform; he wrote it to inspire. It was aimed at the heart. It was a call to action. And it worked.

In April 1861, within days of the Southern army attacking Fort Sumter in South Carolina, Northerners did act. In Boston, three thousand men responded so quickly they were called the "Minute Men of '61."

Among those who reported for duty were two of Paul Revere's grandsons. In Acton, fifty-two men signed up to fight. In Lexington, "several men . . . volunteered," and at the town meeting, citizens voted to spend four thousand dollars to help "the families of those who should enter the service." And in Concord, on April 19, 1861 (of all days!), the artillery company mustered and, as one local writer put it, went "forth to fight our country's battles as our fathers did in '75."

These men from Massachusetts joined others from Maine, New Hampshire, Vermont, Rhode Island, Connecticut, New York, Pennsylvania, New Jersey (where another Revere grandson enlisted), and Delaware. In July 1861, they went to war against a Southern confederacy determined to keep slavery and its plantation economy. In addition to nearly a million fighters, the Confederacy had a president, Jefferson Davis; a White House; a capital city in Richmond, Virginia; and plenty of money.

On January 1, 1863, President Lincoln reversed his earlier position, and with the stroke of a pen, he freed "well over three million" enslaved men, women,

Nosy Neighbor

Two of Paul Revere's grandsons, Edward Hutchinson Revere and Paul Joseph Revere, died fighting for the Union army in the Civil War. Another grandson, Joseph Warren Revere, became a brigadier general and lived until 1880.

Charles Appleton Longfellow, Henry and Fanny's firstborn, enlisted in 1863 and served as a second lieutenant in the First Massachusetts Cavalry.

While stationed in Virginia, Charley got sick and went home to recover. He spent a month at the family's summer house in Nahant, Massachusetts, where he liked to go skinny dipping. Nahant was not quite as secluded as he remembered. The wife of General John C. Fremont, a recent presidential candidate, was summering nearby. Mrs. Fremont had Charley arrested for public nudity. Charley's lawyer won the case because Mrs. Fremont admitted that she needed opera glasses to identify young Longfellow. Charley returned to his army unit, only to be wounded. The bullet just missed his heart and lung and nicked his spine. He lost a lot of blood, but he survived and lived until 1893.

and children in the Southern states (or parts of those states) still in rebellion against the United States. (Although not all enslaved people received notice of their freedom until more than two years later, on June 19, 1865, now known as Juneteenth.) Though Lincoln was still reluctant to offer unqualified freedom to all four million enslaved people in the country, his Emancipation Proclamation also declared that former enslaved people "of suitable condition will be received into the armed service of the United States to garrison the forts . . . and to man vessels of all sorts." When Longfellow saw the first Civil War regiment of black soldiers march down Beacon Street in Boston, he wrote, "an imposing sight, with something wild and strange about it, like a dream. At last the North consents to let the Negro fight for freedom."

Two years later, on April 9, 1865, at Appomattox, Virginia, the Confederate general-in-chief, Robert E. Lee, surrendered, and the United States remained one nation.

Storming Fort Wagner *is an 1890 lithograph by Kurz & Allison depicting one of many Civil War battles.*

"The stupendous news," wrote Longfellow, "almost takes one's breath away." Eight months later, in December 1865, twenty-seven (of the then thirty-six) states ratified the Thirteenth Amendment to the United States Constitution, which abolished slavery as it existed prior to 1863. The amendment stated, "Neither slavery nor involuntary servitude, except as a punishment for crime . . . shall exist within the United States." (Sadly those six words in the middle of the amendment—"except as punishment for a crime"—have been used (and still are) to oppress Black people. How? Police arrest them for petty crimes and judges sentence them to labor in prison. But this is a topic for another book.)

In a few short years, the nation's political institutions took on a whole new look. By 1875, there were Black people serving in both the United States Senate and the House of Representatives. Across the South, hundreds of African Americans held seats in state legislatures, and in 1872, Louisiana elected the first Black governor in American history. Historian Eric Foner calls it a "political revolution."

But many Southern white people refused to accept this new reality. The governor of North Carolina said that allowing Black people to vote would undermine civilization. "In some parts of the south," writes Foner, "armed whites blocked Black people from going to vote or prevented polls from opening on election day." In 1866, a white-hooded hate group called the Ku Klux Klan began spreading what one Alabama man called "a nameless terror among negroes." President Andrew Johnson, who became president after President Lincoln was assassinated, was all for reuniting the nation as long as the Southern states could govern themselves. Many states created laws known as "Black Codes" in order to ensure that formerly enslaved people could work only as field hands or servants and never climb out of poverty. President Johnson vetoed two federal bills that would have allowed Black people to acquire land and start schools.

Former Union army general Ulysses S. Grant succeeded Johnson in 1869. Hoping to reverse Johnson's policies and quell Ku Klux Klan attacks, President Grant sent federal troops (and lots of lawyers) to North Carolina, South Carolina, and Mississippi. The violence abated, but only for a short time in a few states. Meanwhile, other racist organizations sprang up all with the same goal: limiting opportunities for Black people and restoring white supremacy. By the time Grant left office in 1877, the push for racial equality halted just twelve years after it had begun.

Longfellow lived long enough to see the nation once again become "a house divided." In 1878, the seventy-one-year-old poet signed one hundred autographs to raise money for what he called "Southern sufferers" in Chattanooga, Tennessee. "It was like fighting the battle all over again," he wrote.

But fight on he did. Longfellow continued donating money to African American churches until the last month of his life. He continued to wish for a United States in which citizens made sacrifices for the public good, a United States that was kinder, gentler, more tolerant, and more integrated. One biographer writes that Longfellow believed that "the true mission of this country is to receive the poor and degraded of all countries and teach them to be men" and that the real danger came "not from the poor, but from the rich and corrupt, who bring the pest not in their ragged clothes, but in their ragged opinions."

Given his big heart, his empathy for people in need, and his love of liberty, what do you say we forgive Longfellow for his historical sins? Can we agree on that?

At the same time, let's marvel at how Longfellow's poem elevated Paul Revere from Boston folk hero to national legend.

In 1871 (ten years after "Paul Revere's Ride" was published), the citizens of North Chelsea, Massachusetts, voted to change the name of their town to Revere.

On April 18, 1875, on the one hundredth anniversary of Revere's ride, in the North End of Boston, the North Church held its first annual lantern-lighting ceremony. Longfellow's three adult daughters watched from a nearby hillside. That ceremony continues today and includes a reading of "Paul Revere's Ride."

In 1878, a massive granite tablet was affixed to the wall of the North Church. It reads:

> *THE SIGNAL LANTERNS OF PAUL REVERE DISPLAYED IN THE STEEPLE OF THIS CHURCH, APRIL 18, 1775, WARNED THE COUNTRY OF THE MARCH OF THE BRITISH TROOPS TO LEXINGTON AND CONCORD.*

In 1883, artist Cyrus Dallin began sculpting the equestrian statue of Revere that now enlivens the plaza between Hanover and Unity Streets in Boston. Revere sitting atop Brown Beauty remains the most photographed sculpture in Boston.

The first full-length biography of Paul Revere was published in 1891. In 1905, composer E. T. Paull published "Paul Revere's Ride: March-Twostep" that included a "grand crescendo scored quadruple fortissimo." In 1914, Thomas Edison produced a silent movie about Revere's ride, and in 1931, Grant Wood created a painting with unique perspective called *The Midnight Ride.*

The cover of the sheet music for a 1905 song called "Paul Revere's Ride: March-Twostep." Listen to the song by searching online.

The copper dome made by Paul Revere in 1802 is still atop the Massachusetts State House in Boston.

Over the years, Paul Revere has become a brand name adorning bags of sugar and coffee, bottles of whiskey, boxes of pizza, copper-clad cookware, life insurance policies, apartment buildings, bus lines, and (of course) home alarm systems. In the 1950 musical *Guys and Dolls*, two gamblers sing about a racehorse named Paul Revere. In 1958, the United States Postal Service put Revere on a twenty-five-cent stamp. (Longfellow got a one-cent stamp in 1940, and he reappeared on a forever stamp in 2007.) A 1960s rock group called itself Paul Revere and the Raiders. By 2010, there were six more American towns named Revere—in Minnesota, Missouri, North Carolina, North Dakota, Pennsylvania, and Washington. There's also a beach, a park, a mall, and countless streets and schools named after the North End silversmith. Revere's house (the oldest in Boston) is a museum; his portrait (by John Singleton Copley) hangs in the Boston Museum of Fine Arts.

If you want to see an example of Revere's artistry, check out the copper dome that he created for the Massachusetts State House in 1802—it's still there. Exactly two hundred years after that glittering dome was hoisted into place, Massachusetts senator Ted Kennedy told a Boston crowd, "One of my earliest memories was being required by my mother to memorize 'Paul Revere's Ride.'"

Kennedy never forgot it, either. We know because when he wanted 1.6 million dollars in federal funds to restore Longfellow's house, he didn't make a call or write a letter. Instead, he stood on the Senate floor and recited "Paul Revere's Ride" to West Virginia senator Robert Byrd, who was chairman of the Senate committee that controlled those federal funds. Guess what Byrd did? He stood up and recited the poem right back at Kennedy. It was the "first senatorial Longfellow poetry slam."

It may not be the last. Listen my children, indeed.

Acknowledgments

For plucking my manuscript from the slush pile, for guiding me through draft after draft, and for bringing to bear her historical knowledge, her editorial acuity, and her keen sense of narrative structure, my thanks to my editor, Karen Boss. For making sure my manuscript landed on Karen's desk, and for urging me to keep writing draft after draft, I thank my manager, Steven Rosen. For her eagle-eyed copyediting, I thank Josette Haddad, and for her elegant design work, thanks to Diane Earley.

Throughout the research and writing process, a great many people were kind enough to share with me their time, their expertise, and their photocopiers. Thanks to Leslie Wilson and Conni Manoli at the Special Collections Room in the Concord Free Public Library; to Tal Nandan and the gang at the New York Public Library; to Micah Hoggatt and Emily Walhout at the Houghton Library at Harvard; to Bruce Kirby, Michelle Krowl, and Suzana Chilaka at the Library of Congress in Washington, DC; to Betsy Boyle at the Massachusetts Historical Society; to Jeff Levin at the Getty Museum; and to public historians Jayne Triber and Mary Babson Fuhrer; and a loud intercontinental thank-you to Londoner Rosalie Spire, who sent me digital copies of correspondence from the British National Archives in Kew.

Thanks also to John Ulrich at the Harvard Student Agencies; Patrick Leehey at the Paul Revere House; Christine Wirth at the Longfellow

House; Kimberly Reynolds at the Boston Public Library; Chris Adde at the Huntington Library in San Marino, California; Professors Karen Givvin and Jim Stigler at UCLA (for sending me all those JSTOR articles); Elaine C. Doran at the Lexington Historical Society; Shannon Hadley at the Historical Society of Pennsylvania; Richard B. Trask at the Danvers Historical Society; Professor Kimberly Monda at Santa Barbara City College; and unnamed archivists at the University of Glasgow Library in Scotland and the Buffalo and Erie County Public Library.

For help with deciphering eighteenth- and nineteenth-century handwriting, my thanks to Ana Shorr. For introducing me to the work of Carl Zellner, thanks to William Welsch. For scouring the archives at the Antiquarian Society in Worcester, Massachusetts, thanks to James Holdstein.

Thanks to a grant from the National Endowment for the Humanities (long may it thrive!), I was able to spend three productive weeks at the Newberry Library in Chicago. That's where this project began way back in the summer of 2009. Little did I realize then how long I'd be living with Revere and Longfellow.

Thanks to the Houghton Library at Harvard for allowing me to quote from both Longfellow's Account Books and his October 13, 1860, draft of "Paul Revere's Ride."

History professors Gary Nash and Robert Gross have been gracious, supportive, and insightful. Anyone studying eighteenth-century Concord inevitably turns to Gross's award-winning book *The Minutemen and Their World*, and anyone studying the American Revolution cannot do without Nash's *The Urban Crucible*. Journalist Frank Snepp has also tendered wise counsel. As one of the last Americans out of Vietnam (in April 1975), Frank knows much about racing from point A to point B without being captured.

Finally, many thanks to Alan Braunstein (who came up with two-thirds of the title of this book); to Professors Robert Metzger and Michael Collier; to my lawyer, Mark Litwak; to all my inspiring history teachers: Sam Hillard, Francis Meredith, John Thomas, Gordon Wood, Jim Paterson, Stephen Graubard, and Peter Mancall (whose Saturday-morning lectures for educators were always a weekend highlight); to my dynamic teaching colleagues: Michelle Conn, Gillian Keller, Liza Smith, Nancy Seid, and Alex Prinstein; to Longfellow scholars Christoph Irmscher and Dana Gioia; to all my Longfellow-reciting fifth-grade students at Marquez Elementary School in Pacific Palisades, California; to Jeremy Hindert, my student who taught me how to take screenshots of primary sources; to my mom and dad, who shared my love of history; to Matt and Jaime; and to my wife and in-house editor, LeeAn. Every writer should be so lucky as to marry a card-carrying Hollywood story analyst. LeeAn marked up every draft and made sure I never wrote "your" when I meant "you're." She also never failed to remind me when to eat, when to sleep, and when it was time to return to the twenty-first century.

Source Notes

Please see the bibliography on pages 125–130 for more information about the cited works. I've also included historical nuggets here that I was unable to squeeze into the main narrative of the book.

Introduction: You'll Thank Me

p. vii: "dirty snowdrift": Hilen, vol. 5, p. 43. After seeing Longfellow's desk, one visitor noted that there were so many unanswered letters that "only a sharp-toothed mouse could get through them in a month's time" (Irmscher, p. 106).

p. vii: "In the A class Primary . . . a word": Pearl, p. 113.

Prologue: Why So Quiet?

p. xvii: When Revere submitted . . . back to him: Revere, *Three Accounts*, introduction, n.p.

p. xvii: "messengers": Gordon, *History*, vol. 1, p. 477.

p. xvii: "travelers": M. O. Warren, vol. 1, p. 184.

p. xvii: "intelligence . . . country militia": H. Adams, p. 292.

p. xvii: "the part played . . . mentioned": Revere, *Three Accounts*, introduction, n.p.

p. xvii: And when Revere died . . . midnight ride: Patrick Leehey, email message to author, December 28, 2017. Leehey, who is research director at the Paul Revere House, wrote, "I do not know of any Revere obituary that mentions the midnight ride."

p. xviii: So Revere was cut from the narrative: Fischer, pp. 327–28. Historian David Hackett Fischer writes that Revere's testimony was not among the depositions circulated by Whig leaders, because "it did not support the American claim that the regulars had started the fighting, and [it] revealed more about the revolutionary movement than Whig leaders wished to be known. There was little room in this interpretation for the careful preparations that lay behind the American alarm system."

p. xviii: "common talk . . . liability": Wheildon, *Revere's Signal Lanterns*, p. 35.

p. xviii: "We needed . . . ever written": Varney, p. 101.

p. xviii, sidebar: In 1685 . . . France: Leehey, pp. 16–18.

p. xix: "having a little leisure" and "some facts . . . Lexington": Revere, *Three Accounts*: To Jeremy Belknap.

p. xix: "incident . . . basis": Buckingham, p. 39.

p. xix: But it just so happened . . . lousy king: ibid., p. 37.

p. xix, sidebar: "To the right honorable . . . near Boston": Irmscher, pp. 132–33.

p. xix, sidebar: At the time . . . Bailey Circus: ibid., p 133.

p. xix, sidebar: "Does . . . nearby?" and "I know . . . neighborhood": ibid., p. 131.

p. xx: He'd also deliver . . . Miles Standish": Wagenknecht, pp. 87–89. Longfellow had a gift for learning languages. On his first trip to Europe, in 1826, he learned to speak French, Spanish, Italian, and a little German. He also learned to read Portuguese. A fellow language professor said that Longfellow "writes and speaks Spanish with a degree of fluency and exactness

which I have known in no other American born of Parents speaking . . . English as their vernacular" (Wagenknecht, p. 87). On his second trip, in 1835, he perfected his German and learned how to read Finnish, Swedish, Danish, Norwegian, and Dutch. He did all this without the aid of easy-to-read textbooks with vocabulary lists and notes. Instead he'd sit down with newspapers, novels, and poetry and "dig out the meaning of each sentence with the aid of a dictionary" (Wagenknecht, p. 88).

p. xx: That last one . . . in London: Brooks, p. 509. A London journalist wrote about Longfellow, "It is literally true that a volume of his poems is found in nearly every English home. There is no one other work so certain to be encountered, [and] there is no living English poet who has half the circle of readers in England that Mr. Longfellow possesses" (*Atlantic Monthly*, p. 256).

p. xx: "From this tower . . . for Concord" and "innumerable pigeons": S. Longfellow, *Life*, vol. 2, p. 352.

p. xxi: A fine example . . . King George III: P. Smith, pp. 268–69. In 1775, the population of the colonies was about 2,500,000, and about 500,000 of those people were loyalists.

p. xxi: Sixty-eight years . . . the place: Wagenknecht, p. 7.

p. xxi: "Where my writing desk . . . table": Tucker-Macchetta, pp. 23–24.

p. xxi: "perhaps in . . . very house": S. Longfellow, *Life*, vol. 1, p. 379.

p. xxi: "its measured . . . on a stormy day": A. Longfellow, "Reminiscences," n.p.

p. xxi, sidebar: "He might . . . dangerous," "Are you . . . name is," "I may . . . Longfellow," and "on having . . . children": Stearns, p. 70.

p. xxii: "kept up . . . long": S. Longfellow, *Life*, vol. 2, p. 381.

p. xxii: "stealing onward . . . life": Hilen, vol. 2, p. 339.

p. xxii: "constantly arranging . . . child": A. Longfellow, "Reminiscences," n.p.

p. xxii: "even closets . . . pails": Fields, p. 27.

p. xxii: "dedicated to . . . fail": A. Longfellow, "Longfellow," p. 405.

p. xxiii: A typical morning . . . Trap: *Longfellow House*, "Discovering," pp. 1, 5. Alice wrote of her father, "He liked to rise early, and for many years he took a long walk every day before breakfast" (A. Longfellow, "Longfellow," p. 405).

p. xxiii: Returning home . . . milk: Eaton, p. 846.

p. xxiii: "he wrote . . . windows": E. Longfellow, p. 14.

p. xxiii: This disturbed Trap . . . vent: *Longfellow House*, "Discovering," pp. 1, 5.

p. xxiii: "There was . . . resented it": E. Longfellow, p. 77.

p. xxiii: "He was fond of elegance" and "that was at all untidy or unattractive": A. Longfellow, "Longfellow," p. 405.

p. xxiii: If roses . . . his lapel: Hilen, vol. 5, p. 409.

p. xxiii: "perfectly erect": A. Longfellow, "Longfellow," p. 405.

p. xxiii: No wonder . . . mail: Irmscher, pp. 106, 132. One morning in 1857, Longfellow signed eighty autographs. In the Houghton Library at Harvard University, there are over 1,300 requests for his signature. And once he told his sister Annie that he had ninety-nine unanswered letters on his desk (Wagenknecht, p. 44).

p. xxiii: No wonder . . . horse car: Wagenknecht, p. 151.

p. xxiii: And no wonder . . . length: Bardeen, p. 44. The offer of one thousand dollars for ten poems was made in 1857. For the sake of comparison, the average American working man made about six hundred dollars a year in 1857; Longfellow's highest salary as a Harvard professor was eighteen hundred dollars a year; and a United States senator was paid six thousand dollars a year in 1857. According to the Bureau of Labor Statistics, one thousand dollars in 1857 would be worth nearly twenty-nine thousand dollars today. And by the way, Longfellow turned down the offer (Johnson, p. 36; Graf, vol. 3, p. 607).

p. xxv: "grossly . . . inaccurate": Fischer, pp. 331–32.
p. xxv: "The facts . . . sketch": Holland, pp. 16–18.
p. xxv: "confined to . . . historic facts" and "When poets . . . restrained": Hudson, vol. 1, p. 171.

Chapter 1: Dr. Warren Gets the Lowdown

p. 1: By mid-April . . . countryside: Frothingham, *Life*, p. 452, n1. Here's how British commander-in-chief General Thomas Gage described the situation in Boston: "On the 8th of April, 1775, an unusual hurry and commotion was perceived among the disaffected. It being on a Sunday morning, Dr. Cooper, a notorious rebel, was officiating in his meeting house, and, on notice given him, pretended sudden sickness, went home, and sent to another clergyman to do his duty in the evening. He, with every other chief of the [rebel] faction, left Boston before night, and never returned to it."

p. 1: He did . . . house calls: Frothingham, *Life*, p. 452. "Warren's friends felt apprehensions for his safety. As one of his students, Dr. [William] Eustis, returned home one evening, he passed a party of [British] officers who appeared to be on the watch; and he advised Warren not to visit his patients that evening. But Warren, putting his pistols in his pocket, replied, 'I have a visit to make to Mrs. ——, in Cornhill, this evening, and I will go at once: come with me.'"

p. 2: Behind closed doors . . . widowed doctor: Forman, p. 185. According to Warren biographer and medical doctor Samuel Forman, "A parade of nubile young women . . . passed through Warren's practice early in 1774, about a year after he became a widower. If one wanted to flirt with Warren . . . a visit to his medical practice afforded opportunities." Most of these women arrived alone, and the treatments Warren prescribed suggest that he viewed most of their complaints as "mild."

p. 2: In the early afternoon . . . crossed Boston Neck: Galvin, p. 109.

p. 2: In April that year . . . town gate: Coburn, p. 14. Frothingham adds that in September 1774, "General Gage . . . began to fortify Boston Neck . . . and soon mounted . . . two twenty-four pounders and eight nine pounders" (Frothingham, *History*, pp. 15–16). "Twenty-four" and "nine" are the weights of the cannonballs.

p. 2, sidebar: "Whigs . . . authority": B. Williams, p. 5.

p. 3: "to familiarize . . . alarm": Mackenzie, pp. 45–46.

p. 3: By late afternoon . . . clerk: Chase, vol. 2, pp. 321–22.

p. 3: Third . . . loyalists: Gross, p. 137. Gross states that Concord had an "absence of an active Tory [or loyalist] opposition," and anyone who "harbored doubts about the American resistance . . . laid low rather than risk the reprisals which Concord's patriots handed out to suspected loyalists."

p. 3: Some eight months . . . to Cambridge: Fischer, p. 44.

p. 6: After that flawless operation . . . another surprise mission: ibid., pp. 82–84.

p. 6: Twice in the past . . . secret march: ibid., pp. 87–88.

p. 6, sidebar: But the plan fizzled . . . and his knee: Langguth, p. 219.

p. 7: A friend . . . was a woman: Gordon, *History*, p. 476. Roxbury clergyman William Gordon wrote that Dr. Warren's spy was "a daughter of liberty unequally yoked in point of politics." "Unequally yoked" is a phrase from the Bible meaning that right and wrong or light and dark cannot be partners. If oxen are unequally yoked, one is stronger than the other, and they go in circles instead of in a straight line.

p. 7: That woman . . . commander: Fischer, p. 96.

p. 7: Mrs. Gage was born . . . eighteen: Alden, p. 44. Alden says we "may safely conjecture" that Gage traveled to [New] Brunswick because he was interested in Miss Kemble.

p. 7: "that her own emotions . . . described": ibid., p. 248.

p. 8: "was betrayed": ibid., p. 244. Alden is citing a note from British general Henry Clinton, in the Clinton Manuscripts. The other officer with suspicions was General Hugh Percy, who knew that Gage had told only two people of the midnight march, and one of them was Percy himself (Winsor, vol. 3, p. 68).

p. 8: "someone very near to him": Fischer, p. 96.

p. 8: Having been in Boston . . . her medical needs: Alden, p. 204.

p. 8: "hoped . . . countrymen": Hutchinson, vol. 1, p. 497.

p. 8: "belong to . . . than history": Alden, p. 247.

p. 8: "highly probable": Fischer, p. 97.

p. 8, sidebar: "I was one . . . soldiers": Revere, *Three Accounts*: To Jeremy Belknap, n.p.

p. 8, sidebar: Four hundred . . . all the gunpowder: Fischer, p. 56.

p. 9: Gage had ordered . . . to Concord: French, *Informers*, p. 32. Gage's orders to the commanding officer, Colonel Francis Smith, read as follows: "A small party on horseback is ordered out to stop all advice of your march getting to Concord before you."

p. 9: Hancock had moved . . . April 7: J. Clarke, *Diary*, n.p.

p. 9: His entourage . . . Quincy: *Warren-Adams Letters*, vol. 1, p. 45. To this letter James Warren added a note dated the next day, April 7, in which he wrote, "H and A [Hancock and Adams] go no more into that Garrison [Boston], the female Connections of the first come out early this morning."

p. 9: Being both a dapper . . . travel light: Allan, p. 80. Hancock was twenty-seven years old when his childless uncle Thomas died and left him eighty thousand pounds (around ten million dollars today), twenty-two thousand acres of New England wilderness, and six ships.

p. 9: Strapped . . . from London: Unger, p. 68, and Allan, p. 80.

p. 9: Samuel Adams . . . April 10: J. Clarke, *Diary*, n.p.

p. 9: "slenderest . . . in Boston": Miller, p. 313.

p. 9: "nearly six feet . . . of thin person": Unger, p. 7.

p. 9: "the humblest walks of life": Wells, vol. 1, p. 341. Adams looked out for those "who wore a leather cap or worsted apron" (Samuel Fallows, *Samuel Adams: A Character Sketch* [Chicago: University Association, 1898], p. 15).

p. 10: "graceful speaker . . . and dignified": Sears, p. 144.

p. 10: "a quavering voice . . . shaky hand": Morrison, p. 192.

p. 10: "frugal . . . in his habits": Wells, vol. 1, p. 202.

p. 10: To make sure . . . coach house: W. Sumner, p. 189.

p. 10: Adams kept no turkeys . . . was falling down: Wells, vol. 2, p. 209.

p. 10: "artful pen": Wells, vol. 1, p. 446. One British governor of Massachusetts "used to damn that Adams" and complain that "every dip of his pen stung like a horned snake" (Wells, vol. 1, p. 443).

p. 10: But leaders . . . and executed: Chase, vol. 2, p. 293. On March 18, 1775, General Gage acknowledged receiving a letter from King George III in which the king ordered Gage to "apprehend Messrs . . . *Adams, Hancock &c.*, and send them over to *England* to be tried." Then the king sent a second letter, which said to ignore the first order and just "hang them in *Boston*" (Force, pp. 386–87).

p. 10: "Our business . . . and Adams": Willard, p. 88. The letter, dated April 23, was written by an officer in Lord Percy's regiment in Boston.

p. 11: Leaving Warren's . . . a smooch: Holland, pp. 10, 37. According to Dawes biographer Henry Holland, Dr. Warren "sent out Dawes at once by the land route over the Neck." And according to Dawes's granddaughter, her grandpa didn't tell his wife where he was going.

Chapter 2: Nothing Iffy About It

p. 13: At this point . . . Joshua: Fischer, pp. 297–98.
p. 13: That's when . . . shoreline: R. Brown, pp. 47–48.
p. 14: In December . . . Tea Party: Fischer, pp. 299–300.
p. 14: "Desired [him] . . . Lexington": Revere, *Three Accounts*: The Deposition: Corrected Copy, n.p.
p. 14: "they were the objects": ibid., To Jeremy Belknap, n.p.
p. 14: "the colony stores": ibid., The Deposition: Corrected Copy, n.p.
p. 14: "returned . . . Charlestown": ibid., To Jeremy Belknap, n.p.
p. 14, sidebar: Beginning in . . . east was Essex: Keightley, vol. 1, p. 7.
p. 15: "I agreed . . . one": Revere, *Three Accounts*: The Deposition: Corrected Copy, n.p.
p. 15: "paper-thin . . . cow horn": Fischer, p. 99.
p. 15: "I left . . . signals": Revere, *Three Accounts*: To Jeremy Belknap, n.p.
p. 15: "known . . . event": Fischer, p. 388n24.
p. 15: There was also . . . sanctuary: Perry, vol. 3, p. 587. A key was necessary because the North Church had recently been closed and its doors locked. The closure resulted from a rift between Reverend Mather Byles, who was a loyalist, and his congregation, many of whom were patriots. Irritated with his pro-British sermons, the patriots told Byles they would "no longer engage one farthing of salary to their minister." Byles said, "I still offered to officiate... but they treated my kind proposal with neglect; They chose rather to shut up the church."
p. 17, sidebar: "You are . . . your souls": Flexner, p. 14.

Chapter 3: Across the Charles

p. 19: Throughout . . . not his thing: Zellner, "Paul Revere's Rowers," p. 1.
p. 19: One of these . . . Bentley: Goss, vol 1, pp. 188–89. The identities of the rowers were not revealed until 1876, when Paul Revere's grandson John named them in a letter to Elbridge Goss, Revere's first biographer.
p. 20: Seeing Revere . . . Hunt's Wharf: Zellner, "Paul Revere's Rowers," p. 4. By digging into the *Talking Books of the Town of Boston* (1780) and the first *Boston Directory* (1780), Zellner discovered Thomas Richardson's occupation and the likely location of Joshua Bentley's house. In Revere's deposition, he said that "he kept a boat," but Zellner says, "It is doubtful that silversmith Revere had any reason to own a boat. Therefore, his boat, like his horse, was probably borrowed with boat builder Bentley as the likely owner." Revere doesn't include this detail in his first two written accounts, because Richardson and Bentley were probably still in British-occupied Boston and would have been arrested had their identities been revealed (Zellner, "Paul Revere's Rowers," p. 1).
p. 20: "something white . . . ground": Drake, vol. 1, p. 117n1.
p. 20: It was a woolen . . . her body: Coburn, pp. 22–23.
p. 20, sidebar: "for assaulting and beating," "six shillings . . . costs," and "to keep . . . behavior": Triber, p. 36.
p. 20, sidebar: "were . . . abused" and "principal actors": Rowe, p. 79.
p. 20, sidebar: "Revere's willingness . . . cause": Triber, p. 36.
p. 21: With the younger . . . tiller: Zellner, "Paul Revere's Rowers," p. 6.
p. 21: "lunar anomaly": Fischer, p. 105.
p. 21: "shrouded . . . shadow": Olson, pp. 182–83.
p. 21: "I was put . . . boat": Revere, *Three Accounts*: The Deposition: Draft, manuscript, n.p. This supports Zellner's argument that it was not Revere's boat. The sentence appears only in Revere's first deposition and only in the handwritten draft. He must have had second thoughts about revealing the existence of someone's "private boat," because he crossed it out, and it was not included in the published version.

p. 21: "visible in semi-darkness" and "well known . . . watermen": Zellner, "Landing," p. 11.
p. 23: He was twenty-three years old . . . the North Church: Sheets, pp. 3–4.
p. 23: "was a man . . . have done": Wheildon, *Signal Lanterns*, p. 35.
p. 23: "primed two . . . the steeple": Sheets, p. 3.
p. 23: Sitting in the parlor . . . Newman's mother: Fischer, p. 100.
p. 23, sidebar: Unlike most . . . three-cornered hat and In 1909, the tea . . . great-great-grandson: Crawford, p. 128.
p. 25: From a bedroom . . . the garden: Sheets, p. 3.
p. 25: "watching the . . . of the troops": Wheildon, *Signal Lanterns*, p. 38.
p. 25, sidebar: Instead of dictating . . . himself: Fischer, p. 85.
p. 25, sidebar: "on a transport . . . harbor": Chase, vol. 2, p. 323.
p. 25, sidebar: Gage gave . . . were marching and why: Barker, p. 31.
p. 25, sidebar: "equip . . . ball": Willard, p. 197.
p. 25, sidebar: "with the utmost silence" and "was instantly . . . bayonet": Belknap, p. 85.

Chapter 4: Seeing the Light

p. 27: Historian Fischer believes . . . two-man operation: Fischer, p. 388.
p. 27: Newman opened . . . seven of his pals: Sheets, p. 4.
p. 28: "Bell Ringer's Agreement" and "ring . . . desire it": Paul Revere Memorial Association, p. 1.
p. 28: "blew the . . . a flame": Fischer, p. 101.
p. 28: One man held . . . not appear as one: Fischer, p. 388. Also author's personal discussion with a docent at the North Church, August 1, 2012.
p. 28, sidebar: "catch . . . wool" and only . . . childhood: Paul Revere Memorial Association, p. 3.
p. 29: Fearful that . . . a few seconds: Chase, vol. 2, p. 327.
p. 29: "a master . . . pacing" and "slowing . . . builds suspense": Gioia, p. 8.
p. 30: Professor Gioia . . . encampment: Gioia, email message to author, Feb. 25, 2017.
p. 30: That's a natural . . . campsite: Archer, p. xvi.
p. 30, sidebar: A British . . . lanterns: Tyler, p. 104.
p. 30, sidebar: "while engaged . . . funeral": Chase, vol. 2, p. 328.
p. 30, sidebar: Mrs. Pulling . . . Paul Revere: ibid., p. 329.
p. 30, sidebar: "cruel usage": Sheets, p. 10.
p. 30, sidebar: George Washington . . . prisoner exchange: McKenzie, pp. 96–97.
p. 31: "remind . . . liberty": Irmscher, email message to author, Feb. 22, 2017.
p. 31: "lyric moment of reflection": Gioia, p. 8.
p. 31: And yes . . . in the dark: Fischer, p. 115.
p. 31: "a decisive . . . cut" and Gioia suspects . . . so boldly: Gioia, p. 9.

Chapter 5: A Very Good Horse

p. 33: At this point . . . dock: Zellner, "Revere's Landing," p. 11.
p. 34: Revere . . . Fish Street: ibid.
p. 35: We know . . . signals: Revere, *Three Accounts*: To Jeremy Belknap, n.p.
p. 35: "what was acting": ibid. Also Frothingham, *Siege*, p. 58.
p. 35: "I . . . a horse": Revere, *Three Accounts*: To Jeremy Belknap, n.p. The horse belonged to a Charlestown chair maker and fisherman named Samuel Larkin. Samuel's son John was a minister, a tea trader, and a patriot. At John's request, Samuel agreed to loan his horse to Revere (Fischer, p. 389).

p. 35: "I set off . . . horse": Revere, *Three Accounts*: To Jeremy Belknap, n.p.
p. 35: "an excellent . . . very fast": Fischer, p. 106.
p. 35: "It was then . . . very pleasant": Revere, *Three Accounts*: To Jeremy Belknap, n.p.
p. 35: "The moon . . . bright": ibid., The Deposition: Corrected Copy, n.p.
p. 35: "two [British] . . . horse back" and "narrow . . . the road": ibid., The Deposition: Draft, n.p.
p. 35: "to see . . . cockades": ibid.
p. 35, sidebar: Just past . . . iron cage: Fischer, p. 10.
p. 36: "upon a full . . . Mystic Road": ibid.
p. 36: The officer . . . ooze: ibid., To Jeremy Belknap, n.p. Revere wrote, "The one who chased me, endeavoring to cut me off, got into a clay pond. . . . I got clear of him."
p. 37: Thanks to historian . . . rum: Chan, p. 61.
p. 38: If you're wondering . . . in December 1773: Fischer, pp. 299–300.
p. 38: "whose door . . . leader was": Gladwell, pp. 56–57.
p. 38: "gunshots . . . ringing of bells": Fischer, p. 140.
p. 38, sidebar: average . . . four gallons a year: Standage, p. 118.
p. 38, sidebar: "a rabbit bite a bulldog": W. Curtis, p. 93.
p. 39: Reverend Edward Brooks . . . rode off: Castle, p. 171.
p. 39: Another Medford man . . . the coast: Fischer, pp. 140–41.
p. 39: For instance, after leaving . . . another midnight rider: Galvin, p. 114.
p. 39: Once Revere determined . . . along his route: Wellman, p. 113. The Harvard-educated Herrick was one of "our heroes of the Revolution," and on the night of April 18, 1775, "he met Paul Revere in his memorable ride, and going in the opposite direction, gave the warning."
p. 39: "swift running water": Marshall, p. 105.
p. 39: They called it . . . "Anatomy": Sutherland, p. 24.
p. 39: Revere woke minutemen . . . rouse their neighbors: Fischer, pp. 125–26.
p. 40: One neighbor . . . liquid into musket balls: Parker, p. 142, and Castle, p. 187.
p. 40: Men . . . arsenal: Powers, p. 225. Powers writes, "Everyone was ready for the soldiers. Even the mothers helped, for they built hot fires and melted their pewter plates and tea urns and sugar bowls and made them into bullets."

Chapter 6: Hello, Mr. Dawes

p. 43: Historians . . . Lexington: Fischer, p. 109.
p. 43: a farming town . . . one tailor: Fuhrer, email message to author, July 1, 2017.
p. 43: The 181 landowning . . . militia: Pruitt, n.p.
p. 44: Hancock and Adams . . . parlor: Fischer, p. 110.
p. 44: Crammed into . . . five to fifteen: Fischer, pp. 108–9, and Kollen, *Letters*, p. 1.
p. 44: As Revere neared . . . disturbed by any noise: Phinney, p. 33.
p. 45: "Noise!" . . . their march": ibid, p. 16.
p. 45: "permitted him to pass": ibid, p. 33.
p. 45: Revere knocked . . . was there," "wished . . . Mr. Hancock," "did not . . . business," and "Come in . . . afraid of you": Phinney, pp. 16–17.
p. 45: After reading it . . . town bell rung: W. Sumner, p. 187.
p. 45: The thing weighed . . . militia: Bartlett, p. 99.
p. 45, sidebar: Every able-bodied . . . town's militia: Gross, p. 59.
p. 45, sidebar: The only exceptions . . . conscientious objectors: Fischer, p. 151.
p. 45, sidebar: Militiamen drilled . . . of their town: "Who Were the Minute Men," National Park Service, last modified February 26, 2015, https://www.nps.gov/mima/learn/education/who-were-the-minute-men.htm.

p. 45, sidebar: About a quarter . . . muster and march: Fischer, p. 152.
p. 46: "I related . . . before me": Revere, *Three Accounts*: To Jeremy Belknap, n.p.
p. 46: Revere went outside . . . Bedford Road: Revere, *Three Accounts*: The Deposition: Corrected Copy, n.p.
p. 46: Earlier at the . . . country bumpkin: Holland, p. 20.
p. 46: Having ridden . . . to Woburn: Hurd, vol. 1, p. 447. Revere mentions no detour to Cambridge, and Stedman's Tavern was just half a block off Dawes's route. It's clear that *someone* brought the alarm to Stedman's, because sometime after midnight, Stedman sent an alarm rider north, and this rider arrived in Woburn around two o'clock in the morning (Fischer, p. 146).
p. 46: "We refreshed ourselves": Revere, *Three Accounts*: To Jeremy Belknap, n.p.
p. 46: The two riders . . . could be found: Tourtellot, p. 100.
p. 46, sidebar: It consisted . . . a scorched flavor: Bacheller, p. 16.
p. 47: Lexington militia commander . . . to alarm Bedford: J. Clarke, *Battle*, p. 54. Also, Phinney, p. 38.
p. 47: In addition . . . four hours earlier: Phinney, p. 31.
p. 47: Before April 19 . . . and Concord: Fischer, p. 146.
p. 47: Behind them . . . well buckets: Bacheller, p. 7, and Fuhrer, pp. 38–39.
p. 47: "I feared . . . mixing came": Bacheller, pp. 7–8. According to Mrs. Munroe, the redcoats ate the bread the following day.
p. 47, sidebar: On the night . . . in Woburn: Castle, p. 314.
p. 47, sidebar: When not engaged . . . Boston Harbor: Fischer, p. 288.
p. 47, sidebar: "woodpeckers . . . tree" and "excellent flavor": Cutter, p. 67.

Chapter 7: Trouble

p. 49: Instead . . . leading questions: Gross, p. 116, and Tourtellot, p. 100.
p. 49: When Prescott's answers . . . for Concord: Revere, *Three Accounts*: To Jeremy Belknap, n.p.
p. 49: "and would . . . credit": ibid.
p. 50: A latch clicked . . . his brother-in-law: MacLean, pp. 265–66, and Fischer, p. 144.
p. 50: "There are two . . . have them": Revere, *Three Accounts*: To Jeremy Belknap, Manuscript, n.p.
p. 50: In full gallop . . . the two soldiers: Fischer, p. 130. Revere wrote, "The Docter . . . came up; and we tried to git past them" (Revere, *Three Accounts*: To Jeremy Belknap, n.p.).
p. 50, sidebar: Nathaniel Baker . . . in 1776: MacLean, p. 265.
p. 51: "God damn . . . dead man": Revere, *Three Accounts*: The Deposition: Corrected Copy, n.p.
p. 51: The patriots . . . pasture: Malcolm, p. 41. The property was owned by William Dodge, but it was called the Jacob Foster farm because Foster was the tenant who "lived on and improved the property" for the Dodges.
p. 51: "Put on.": Revere, *Three Accounts*, The Deposition: Corrected Copy, n.p.
p. 51: Prescott raced . . . clean away: ibid., The Deposition: Draft, n.p.
p. 51: Dawes reached . . . Lexington: Holland, p. 35.
p. 51: "intending . . . that" and "and run afoot": Revere, *Three Accounts*, The Deposition: Draft, n.p.
p. 52: "out started . . . officers": ibid., The Deposition: Corrected Copy, n.p.
p. 52: They rode . . . he did: ibid., The Deposition: Draft, n.p.
p. 52: "was an express" and "I answered in the affirmative": ibid., To Jeremy Belknap, n.p.
p. 52: The soldier . . . come from: ibid., The Deposition: Draft, n.p.
p. 52: "I came . . . come out": Phinney, p. 32.
p. 52: "would miss their aim" and "I told . . . knew better" and "I knew . . . there soon": Revere, *Three Accounts*, The Deposition: Draft, n.p.
p. 52: "Sir, may I . . . Yes" and "abused me much": ibid., n.p.

p. 52, sidebar: "There are two . . . them": Revere, *Three Accounts*: To Jeremy Belknap, Manuscript, n.p.
p. 53: Mitchell "clapped his pistol . . . brains out": ibid., To Jeremy Belknap, n.p.
p. 53: "When I had mounted" and "the Major . . . lead me": ibid., The Deposition: Draft, n.p.
p. 53: Major Mitchell . . . "countrymen" . . . the bushes: ibid.
p. 53: The others . . . toward Concord and "inquired . . . Adams were": Phinney, pp. 31–32.
p. 53: "many more . . . particular": Revere, *Three Accounts*: The Deposition: Draft, n.p.
p. 53: "A quarter . . . o'clock": Phinney, p. 31.
p. 53: With the patriots . . . the soldier, "pretty smart," "damned rebel," "critical situation," "a gun fired," "cut the . . . their business," and "When we . . . guns fired": Revere, *Three Accounts*: The Deposition: Draft, n.p.
p. 55: "and asked . . . was tired" and "Take . . . man's horse": ibid., To Jeremy Belknap, n.p.
p. 55: "They told . . . towards Cambridge": ibid., The Deposition: Draft, n.p.
p. 55: "alarmed . . . Lexington": ibid.

Chapter 8: Dr. Prescott Rides On

p. 57: The right guy . . . named Sukey: MacLean, p. 268.
p. 57: After hearing . . . Lincoln minutemen: Malcolm, p. 56.
p. 57: He was a farmer . . . Concordian: Luzader, pp. 1–2.
p. 57: "John, the bell's . . . the village": Chase, vol. 3, p. 4.
p. 58: Since all three . . . horses: Tax Records, n.p.
p. 58: The warnings . . . southeast to Natick: Castle, p. 261, and Fischer, p. 146.
p. 58: Massachusetts colonists . . . in 1676: Kollen, *Liberty's Birthplace*, p. 21.
p. 58: Because a year . . . countryside: Bancroft, vol. 2, p. 98. Bancroft writes about Native Americans being "crowded by hated neighbors, losing fields and hunting grounds" and waking "to the danger of extermination." Historians Eric Schultz and Michael Tougias write, "It is impossible to escape the fact that New England Indians were victims of colonial Americans' inexhaustible appetite for territory and expansion" (Schultz and Tougias, p. 18).
p. 58: To defend their villages . . . and Plymouth: Schultz and Tougias, pp. 2–3. Like the Iroquois in upstate New York, the Wampanoag, Nipmuc, Narragansett, and Pocumtuck were confederacies that included various sub-tribes related by "a common linguistic tradition" (Schultz and Tougias, p. 11).
p. 58: This ninety-nine . . . Cambridge: Fischer, p. 139.
p. 58: Back in Concord . . . barrels: Ryan, p. 91. Ryan also mentions fifteen-year-old Melicent Barrett, who spent the night of April 18 and 19 rolling and preparing powder cartridges that were most likely fired at the regulars the next day (ibid., p. 92).
p. 59: That included not only . . . barrels of beef!: Shattuck, pp. 97–98.
p. 59: At his home . . . locked the door: Coburn, pp. 91–92.
p. 59: On Main Street . . . feather bed: Chase, vol. 3, p. 18. Also, Mary R. Fenn, *Old Houses of Concord*. Concord: Old Concord Chapter of the D.A.R., 1974, p. 26.
p. 59, sidebar: One of the men . . . enslaved black man: Kollen, *Liberty's Birthplace*, p. 31.
p. 59, sidebar: In 1775 . . . population: Manegold, p. 75.
p. 59, sidebar: "a negro boy": Manegold, p. 209.
p. 59, sidebar: "A slave . . . house": Wells, vol. 1, p. 138.
p. 59, sidebar: "denounce . . . slaveholding": Gross, p. 97.
p. 59, sidebar: Revere never . . . either: Jayne Triber, email message to author, April 23, 2018. Triber discovered a letter written in 1785 that suggests that Revere was opposed to slavery.

The letter was written by Thomas Wadsworth, a friend of Revere's who had moved to South Carolina, where he became a slave-owning plantation owner. Revere's letter to Wadsworth has not been found, but it must have been critical, because Wadsworth replied, "I have nothing to say on that subject . . . but don't ask me any more of these questions." Interestingly, in his will, Wadsworth freed his enslaved people. Perhaps Revere had something to do with that.

p. 59, sidebar: In 1781 . . . for freedom: Zilversmit, p. 614.

p. 59, sidebar: Two years . . . abolished slavery": ibid., p. 615.

p. 60: In the northern . . . manure: ibid., p. 7. Also M. Barrett, p. 64.

p. 60: When the cart . . . boughs: ibid., p. 6.

p. 60: In response . . . needed: Fischer, p. 128.

p. 60: Colonel Smith . . . to arrive: ibid., p. 127. In his report to General Gage, Colonel Smith wrote, "When I had got some miles on the march from Boston I detached six light infantry companies to march with all expedition to seize the two bridges on different roads beyond Concord" (K. G. Davies, ed., *Documents of the American Revolution, 1770–1783*, Colonial Office series [Dublin: Irish University Press, 1975], vol. 9, p. 103).

p. 61: It was around three . . . burying ground: Phinney, p. 31. Recall that Sanderson testified that it was quarter after two in the morning when he, Revere, and the other prisoners left Foster's pasture and headed back to Lexington. Given the distances involved, three o'clock seems a reasonable estimate.

p. 61: Turns out . . . militia: W. Sumner, p. 187.

p. 61: Samuel Adams . . . ride a horse: *Warren-Adams Letters*, vol. 1, pp. 110–11.

p. 61: Over the next hour . . . sword: W. Sumner, p. 187.

p. 61: Hancock's aunt Lydia . . . leave: Chase, vol. 2, p. 347.

p. 61, sidebar: "skill . . . statesman," "gracefully . . . side," and "defended . . . injury": *Warren-Adams Letters*, pp. 110–11.

p. 62: "If I had . . . these troops": Phinney, p. 34.

p. 62: "[Fighting] is not . . . cabinet": Chase, vol. 2, p. 347.

p. 62: "I wish you . . . please him": Harrington, p. 266.

p. 62: Tavern keeper . . . in Woburn: Phinney, p. 34.

p. 62: The new hideout . . . Woburn minister: Chase, vol. 2, p. 347.

p. 62: The late Reverend . . . in Lexington: Varney, p. 99. Quite a few Massachusetts religious leaders were patriots. In addition to Clarke in Lexington and Jones in Woburn, patriot clergy included Reverends Thomas Allen of Pittsfield, Henry Cumings of Billerica, Philip Payson of Chelsea, Peter Thatcher of Malden, and John Treadwell of Lynn (Baldwin, pp. 185–88). Once the war began, more than sixty New England ministers served the patriot cause in some nonmilitary capacity, and many became political leaders. This really bugged some of the loyalists. One of them, Daniel Leonard of Taunton, protested that "when clergy engage in political warfare, religion becomes a most powerful engine." Another loyalist, Peter Oliver from Middleborough, labeled patriot clergymen "the black regiment," referring both to their robes and to their "evil intent" (Kollen, *Patriot*, p. 70).

p. 62: Revere . . . a fish: W. Sumner, p. 188, and Fischer, p. 179.

p. 62: The trunk . . . patriot documents: Revere, *Three Accounts*: The Deposition: Draft, n.p.

p. 63: As they neared . . . two miles: ibid., The Deposition: Corrected Copy, n.p. Militiaman Joseph Underwood testified that "the first certain information we had of the approach of the British troops was given by Thaddeus Bowman between four and five o'clock on the morning of the 19th" (Phinney, p. 39). Just as Revere had done earlier, Bowman wheeled his horse to elude capture by two British soldiers "concealed along the side of the road" (Sabin, p. 31).

p. 63: "beat the . . . to arms": Tourtellot, p. 113. In some historical accounts, including Tourtellot's, William Diamond's age is given as sixteen, but on his tombstone (in Peterborough, New Hampshire) and on his Revolutionary War pension application, his birthday is listed as July 21, 1755, which would've made him nineteen (Kollen, *Treasures*, p. 120). Diamond's drum survived the skirmish and the war and can be seen today in the Hancock-Clarke house (ibid., p. 119).

p. 63: Joining Diamond . . . year before: Lossing, p. 18.

p. 63: "hurried . . . meeting-house," "lights moving," and "I fifed . . . might": ibid., p. 19.

p. 63: "Every man . . . company": Ripley, p. 53.

p. 63–4: "There are so few . . . here" and "The first . . . shot down": ibid., p. 52.

p. 64: There was also . . . by marriage: Wood, p. 45.

p. 64: While these militiamen . . . stairs: Revere, *Three Accounts*: To Jeremy Belknap, n.p. As Revere put it, he and Lowell went "up chamber."

p. 64: Hancock's . . . feet high: Fischer, p. 181.

p. 64: "chamber window": Revere, *Three Accounts*: The Deposition: Draft, n.p.

p. 64: "coming up the road": ibid., n.p.

p. 64: Continuing across . . . or sixty and "Let the troops . . . them": ibid., The Deposition: Corrected Copy, n.p.

p. 64: "an army of observation": Gross, p. 112. In Captain Parker's defense, he may have felt he was simply following the March 30, 1775, resolution of the Massachusetts Provincial Congress. It stated that whenever General Gage sent five hundred or more soldiers, with artillery and baggage, into the countryside, "the [colonial] military force of the province ought to be assembled, and an Army of Observation immediately formed, to act solely on the defensive." To be clear, British commander Francis Smith brought with him no artillery, but Parker didn't know that (French, *Day*, p. 41).

p. 64: In the front . . . Jesse Adair: French, *Informers*, pp. 43, 48, and Fischer, p. 127.

p. 64: "brave, but brainless": Fischer, p. 282. Adair's brainlessness was on full display in March 1776 when the British army left Boston. It was assumed that the patriots would attack the last soldiers to evacuate. Lieutenant Adair was ordered to slow the advance of the patriots by strewing razor-sharp iron devices called crow's feet in the street. Stepping on one of these "could cripple a man or a horse." An English officer recalled that Adair scattered the crow's feet "from the gate *toward* the enemy," meaning that he "had to walk over them on his return, which detained him so long that he was nearly taken prisoner" (Hunter, p. 15).

p. 64: "quick to act . . . understand": Fischer, p. 189.

p. 64–5: No surprise . . . Lexington and Seeing the front . . . patriot militiamen: French, *Informers*, p. 48.

p. 65: "Stand your ground!": Coburn, p. 63.

p. 65: "Disperse . . . rebels!": Phinney, p. 37.

p. 65: "Lay down . . . arms!": Fischer, p. 191.

p. 65: "You . . . run!": Phinney, p. 37. According to historian Douglas Sabin, "It is easy to imagine the hot-tempered [Major Edward] Mitchell assuming the role of the angry belligerent on Lexington Common," and "it is possible . . . that Mitchell . . . played a larger role in the tragedy than history will record." One British soldier heard that, in Lexington, after the patriot line broke, "Mitchell and seven or eight officers charged them" (Sabin, p. 48).

p. 65: Captain Parker may have . . . of rebels: Galvin, p. 124.

p. 65: "continual . . . musketry": Revere, *Three Accounts*: To Jeremy Belknap, n.p.

p. 65: "flying thick about him" and "into a wood . . . hour": Gordon, "Account," p. 628.

p. 65: "was continued . . . seen": Shattuck, p. 350.

Chapter 9: First Blood

p. 67: "saw . . . troops": Revere, *Three Accounts*: The Deposition: Corrected Copy, n.p.
p. 67: "gave . . . fired": ibid., n.p.
p. 67: "the angry . . . regulars" and "fired his . . . shoot": Lossing, p. 19. This version of events is corroborated by a British soldier who said, "It was the talk among the soldiers that Major Pitcairn fired his pistol, then drew his sword, and ordered them to fire" (Gordon, "Account," p. 627).
p. 67: "God damn . . . them!": Harrington, p. 261.
p. 67: "fired . . . soldiers" and "begin a scattered fire": French, *Informers*, p. 53.
p. 68: Eight patriots . . . retreating rebels: Galvin, p. 128.
p. 68: Riding onto . . . the carnage: Fischer, p. 198.
p. 68: "desirous of . . . deluded people": French, *Informers*, p. 62.
p. 68: "We then . . . no orders": Barker, p. 32.
p. 68: "three hazzas": J. Clarke, *Battle*, p. 59.
p. 68, sidebar: A 1775 print . . . no militiamen disperse: Murdock, pp. 6–8.
p. 68, sidebar: The town of Lexington . . . Town Hall: Kollen, *Liberty's Birthplace*, p. 126.
p. 69: "to destroy . . . collected there": Barker, p. 32.
p. 69: "being alarmed . . . assembling," "impracticable," and "advised . . . return to Boston": Mackenzie, p. 63.
p. 69: "listened politely": Fischer, p. 200.
p. 69: "determined to . . . had received": Mackenzie, p. 63.
p. 70: Revere went in . . . the potatoes: B. Clarke, p. 91.
p. 70: Aunt Lydia . . . the barn and "one . . . behaved better": W. Sumner, p. 188.
p. 70, sidebar: "We are . . . surrounded!" and "Clear that house!": A. Brown, p. 33.
p. 70, sidebar: Simonds lived . . . thirty years: ibid.
p. 71: "a messenger . . . rushed in," "hotly pursued," and Hancock ordered . . . conceal it: Varney, p. 99.
p. 71: "piloted" and "by a cart-way": Woodbury, p. 67.
p. 71: "in an obscure corner . . . Billerica" and Missing his fresh . . . and potatoes: Varney, p. 99.
p. 71: Later . . . a cow: ibid., p. 100.

Chapter 10: "For God's Sake, Fire!"

p. 73: first to fall . . . Acton minutemen: Gross, p. 125.
p. 74: clear skies . . . in the morning: Fischer, p. 311.
p. 74: The regulars . . . held the North Bridge and As for the patriots . . . John Buttrick's place: Galvin, pp. 140–42. Also Fischer, p. 314.
p. 74: seventy-seven from Bedford: Castle, p. 43.
p. 74: sixty-two from Lincoln: Coburn, p. 81.
p. 74: ninety or so from Acton: Castle, p. 27.
p. 74: sixteen from Carlisle and Billerica: ibid., p. 81.
p. 74: nine from Groton: Wheildon, *New Chapter*, p. 5.
p. 74: four from Westford: Castle, p. 302.
p. 74: "several squads . . . and Stow": Galvin, p. 144.
p. 74: "a formidable force": Sutherland, p. 20.
p. 74: A spark . . . burned, too: Sabin, p. 75.
p. 74, sidebar: Isaac Davis . . . April 19 and "asleep in his bed": J. Adams, p. 47.

p. 75: "I have . . . it is true": Hosmer, n.p.

p. 75: "Will you . . . town?": ibid. A Tory who didn't know Joseph Hosmer once asked of him, "How comes he to speak such pure English?" The response was, "Because he has an old mother who sits in the chimney corner and reads English poetry all day long, and I suppose it is, 'like mother, like son'" (Gross, pp. 64–65).

p. 75: Captain William Smith . . . from the bridge: A. Brown, p. 109.

p. 75, sidebar: While there was . . . name on them: Shattuck, p. 229. Also Bacheller, p. 20.

p. 75, sidebar: A fire warden . . . was fined: Bacheller, p. 20.

p. 76: All winter . . . eight times a month: Galvin, p. 52.

p. 76: "in the large . . . of the parsonage": Drake, vol. 2, p. 277. Writing in 1880, Drake says that gun marks in the ceiling of the parsonage were "recently repaired."

p. 76: In Acton . . . twice a week: J. Adams, p. 43.

p. 76: "inform . . . firelocks" and "non appearance": Castle, p. 314.

p. 76: And in Concord . . . fire a cannon: Revolutionary-Era Concord Town Records, January 9, 23, and 27, 1775.

p. 77: "march . . . attempt": Shattuck, p. 111.

p. 77: "Many had done . . . their muskets": Fischer, p. 209. "Double-shotted" is what it sounds like: loading a gun with two musket balls and extra gunpowder. During the firefight in Lexington, John Munroe double-shotted his musket and later testified that "on firing at the British the strength of the charge took off about a foot of my gun barrel" (Phinney, p. 36). John Munroe's foreshortened musket can be seen today in the barroom of the Munroe Tavern, a museum located in Lexington, Massachusetts (Bacheller, p. 17).

p. 77: Before they marched . . . fire first: Ripley, p. 25. Lincoln minuteman Amos Barrett also recalled "strict orders not to fire 'till they fired first" (True, p. 33).

p. 77: "Let every single . . . action": French, *Day*, p. 204.

p. 77: Those men had no bayonets: Rantoul, p. 134. In his affidavit, Amos Baker said, "When we were going to march down to the Bridge, it was mentioned between Major Buttrick and Captain Isaac Davis that the [Acton] minute-men had better be put in front, because they were the only men that had bayonets, and it was not certain whether the British would fire, or whether they would charge bayonets without firing. I do not remember which of them said it, but both agreed to it; and Captain Davis's company of minute-men was then brought up on the right" (ibid.).

p. 77: Buttrick hurried . . . every one of his minutemen: Castle, p. 28.

p. 78: "with a[s] much order . . . troops": Lister, p. 27.

p. 78: "unable to march": French, *Day*, p. 165. When first offered the job as Concord's commanding officer, James Barrett turned it down, saying he was too old. But influential citizens pressed him and promised, "all they wanted of him was his advice." But on April 19, he was giving a lot more than advice.

p. 78: "rode nearer . . . companies": Sabin, p. 79.

p. 78: A group . . . Barrett's horse: N. Barrett, n.p.

p. 78: Ahead they could see . . . long before: Luzader, p. 2. Luzader writes that John Buttrick "frequently performed work on . . . the North Bridge."

p. 78: When Buttrick . . . tearing up the planks: Fischer, p. 210.

p. 78: "desisted and formed for action": J. Adams, p. 45.

p. 78: "drive them away from the bridge": True, p. 33.

p. 78, sidebar: "crazy man": Emerson, p. 75.

p. 78, sidebar: "incapable of . . . business": Gross, p. 83.

p. 78, sidebar: "may have been . . . town": Fischer, p. 216.
p. 79: Buttrick gave . . . bridge: J. Adams, p. 44.
p. 79: "Their balls whistled well": True, p. 33.
p. 79: "a general popping . . . ensued" and "gave afire": French, *Informers*, p. 97.
p. 79: "His blood . . . clothes": A. Brown, p. 164. Acton man Thomas Thorp said that "wherever he went in the long war that followed, he seemed to see Davis's blood . . . urging him to do his duty" (Chase, vol. 3, p. 36).
p. 79: Even in death . . . hand: A. Brown, p. 164.
p. 79: Joshua Brooks . . . his hat: MacLean, p. 274.
p. 79: So did Acton's . . . captain and Abner Hosmer . . . fell dead: J. Adams, p. 44.
p. 79: "Fire . . . fire!": Ripley, p. 27.
p. 79: "fired his own piece": French, *Day*, p. 191.
p. 79: With the balls . . . other way: N. Barrett, n.p. Young Barrett wrote that he "stayed until he saw Captain Davis and others fall [and] then thought it would be best for him to go home."
p. 79: "received a shot . . . half round": Sutherland, p. 21.
p. 79: "like a flock of sheep": Emerson, p. 75.
p. 79: "It was not . . . ceased": Varney, p. 87.
p. 80: "There was eight . . . after them": True, p. 33.
p. 80: "back of Elisha Jones's house": J. Adams, p. 45. After hearing the shooting, Colonel Smith led "two companies of grenadiers" toward the North Bridge. He stopped about two hundred yards south of the bridge, where he met "the broken remnants" of Captain Laurie's detachment. Smith also saw the two hundred patriots Major Buttrick had positioned on the high ground behind Elisha Jones's house. Smith consulted with his officers, then gave the order to fall back (Fischer, p. 215).
p. 81: A few even left for home: Fischer, p. 214. When a Concord woman spotted one of the patriot fighters leaving, she called to him that he should leave his gun. The man disagreed and continued walking. The woman shouted, "No, stop. I must have it." The man started to run. The woman took off after him, but "he got away and she gave up the chase" (N. Barrett, n.p.).
p. 81: "After the fire . . . commander": Varney, p. 87.
p. 81: Several men . . . house: Rantoul, p. 135. Mrs. Davis recalled that her husband's body was brought home to Acton in the afternoon and placed in her bedroom until the funeral. "His countenance was pleasant, and seemed little altered," she said (J. Adams, p. 47).
p. 81: Colonel Barrett sent . . . his house: Fischer, p. 215.
p. 81: "a bushel of doughnuts": Prescott, p. 5.
p. 81: In the center . . . nearby houses: Chase, vol. 3, p. 52.
p. 81: "It was owing . . . taken prisoners": J. Adams, p. 45.
p. 82: "assumed any command": ibid., p. 44.
p. 82: "to attack . . . without cause": Fischer, p. 216.
p. 82: "the first British . . . Revolutionary War": Sabin, p. 91.
p. 82: He had no way . . . empty apartment: *Detail and Conduct*, p. 10. This botching of the rescue operation is described in a letter sent from Boston dated July 4, 1775. The unknown letter writer said that on the night of April 18, one of General Gage's subordinates sent out letters to the two officers assigned to assemble the reinforcements. Those two officers were ordered to have their soldiers ready to go at four o'clock on the morning of the nineteenth. One of the two officers came home late on the eighteenth, went right to bed, and never read the orders. He had to be awakened the next morning at five thirty, and his men finally assembled at six o'clock. The other officer to whom an order was sent was Major John Pitcairn. The letter

writer apparently didn't realize that Pitcairn had been sent on the march to Concord. So the Royal Marines assigned to General Percy's rescue force didn't assemble for another two hours. The letter writer says, "This double mistake lost us from four till nine o'clock, the time we marched off to support Col. Smith."

p. 82: "ordered his . . . formation": Sabin, p. 107.
p. 82: Flankers assigned . . . the south: Galvin, p. 165.
p. 82: "We found them . . . after them": True, p. 33.
p. 82: These patriots . . . on spring break: Castle, p. 223.
p. 83: "just at . . . to Concord," "going to . . . the answer," and "borrowed accoutrement": Ripley, pp. 32–33.
p. 83: "the mournful creak . . . carriages": Fischer, p. 220.
p. 83: "silence reigned on both sides": Ripley, p. 33.
p. 83: As the first . . . and fired back: Fischer, p. 220.
p. 83: Their balls flew high: Ripley, p. 33.
p. 83: "This ineffectual . . . little from it": Mackenzie, p. 66.
p. 83: "returned fire . . . accuracy": Fischer, p. 220.
p. 83: Two British . . . near the brook: Sabin, p. 120.
p. 83: "the ball . . . within the skin": Lister, p. 31.

Chapter 11: Battle Road

p. 85: "It . . . hedges and walls": Lister, p. 29.
p. 85: "They were . . . seeing them": French, *Day*, p. 223.
p. 85: As the regulars slogged . . . from Framingham: Coburn, pp. 96–97.
p. 85: 104 from Chelmsford: Castle, p. 86.
p. 85: 101 from Billerica: ibid., p. 96.
p. 85: 33 from Tewksbury: Hurd, vol. 3, p. 294.
p. 85: "Stand trim . . . elbows off": ibid.
p. 85: "landscape was . . . of flame": G. Curtis, p. 106. When the regulars reached the Lincoln town line, the patriots had a force of over fifteen hundred men (Coburn, p. 97).
p. 86: "The rebels . . . side": Force, p. 441.
p. 86: "the fire . . . never slackened": Sutherland, p. 22.
p. 86: "I had my hat . . . my bayonet": Force, p. 440.
p. 86: "Ingeniously . . . in detail": Gioia, p. 10.
p. 86: During the fighting . . . just 94: Fischer, p. 321.
p. 86: "a dish of tea" and "It is beyond . . . that tea": Lister, p. 34.
p. 86, sidebar: "hasty pudding and milk": A. Brown, pp. 225–26.
p. 87: In his official . . . alarm system: Carter, vol. 2, p. 674. Gage wrote, "It appears from the firing of alarm guns and ringing of bells, that the march of Lieutenant Colonel Smith was discovered, and he was opposed by a body of men within six miles of Concord. The whole country was assembled in arms with surprising expedition."
p. 87: "timeless emblem . . . independence": Gioia, p. 11. Similarly, Professor Angela Sorby writes that the poem "is energized by a streak of magical thinking that knits the local to the national, the temporal to the timeless, and the living to the dead" (Sorby, p. 15).
p. 88: It was probably . . . Committee of Safety: Revere, *Three Accounts*: to Jeremy Belknap, n.p.
p. 88: At this volatile . . . governing authority: Fischer, p. 266.
p. 88: During a . . . and underwear: Goss, vol. 1, p. 263.
p. 88: On that same . . . of Safety: Revere, *Three Accounts*: to Jeremy Belknap, n.p.

p. 88: "to defend our wives . . . inhuman soldiery": Frothingham, *Life*, p. 466.
p. 88, sidebar: Armed with a musket . . . Cooper's Tavern: Tourtellot, 197.
p. 88, sidebar: A pistol shot . . . later died: Coburn, p. 142.
p. 88, sidebar: "We killed an old devil . . . for it": S. Smith, p. 44.
p. 88, sidebar: Whittemore's blood-soaked . . . wounds: ibid., p. 43.
p. 88, sidebar: Wouldn't you know . . . eighteen years: ibid., pp. 43–44.
p. 89: "expenses for self and horse": O'Brien, p. 37. The Committee of Safety thought five shillings a day was too high, so they reduced it to four.

Chapter 12: American Mythology

p. 91: "In glorifying Paul Revere . . . well-earned honors": Murdock, p. 5.
p. 92: "the great truth . . . white man" and "slavery . . . condition": Schott, p. 334. These ideas were expressed by Alexander Stephens, the vice president of the Confederacy. They are taken from his so-called Cornerstone Speech, delivered in Savannah, Georgia, in March 1861.
p. 92: "I have always . . . abolitionist": Basler, vol. 2, p. 492.
p. 92: "free labor on free soil": Dray, p. 70.
p. 92: "Compromise . . . surrender": Hilen, vol. 4, p. 214.
p. 92: Longfellow wanted the president . . . nation: C. Sumner, *Works*, vol. 5, pp. 18–19. Longfellow agreed with his eloquent friend Senator Charles Sumner, who had this to say about the evils of slavery: "The slave is held simply for the use of his master, to whose behests his life, liberty and happiness are devoted, and by whom he may be bartered, leased, mortgaged, bequeathed, invoiced, shipped as cargo, stored as goods, sold on execution, knocked off at public auction and even staked at the gaming table on the hazard of a card or die; all according to law. Nor is there anything, within the limit of life, inflicted on the beast which may not be inflicted on the slave. He may be marked like a hog, branded like a mule, yoked like an ox, hobbled like a horse, driven like an ass, sheared like a sheep, maimed like a cur and constantly beaten like a brute; all according to law."
p. 92: "this land," "whips and yokes," and "insult humanity": H. W. Longfellow, *Poems*, p. 10. The poem referred to here is "To William Channing." William Ellery Channing was one of the most outspoken abolitionists of the 1830s. He died in 1842.
p. 92: "unrighteous . . . right": S. Longfellow, *Life*, vol. 2, p. 8.
p. 93: But during the 1850s . . . in Boston: ibid., pp. 192–93. Here's a journal entry from April 4, 1851: "There is much excitement in Boston about the capture of an alleged fugitive slave. O city without soul! When and where will this end? Shame, that the great Republic, the 'refuge of the oppressed,' should stoop so low as to become the Hunter of Slaves." Here's another entry from June 2, 1854: "The fugitive slave is surrendered to his master. . . . Dirty work for a country that is so loud about freedom as ours" (ibid., p. 246).
p. 93: In his letters . . . slaveholders: ibid., pp. 247, 281. On June 2, 1854, Longfellow wrote to Sumner: "This morning I have read your last . . . speech. It is one of your best, with a pulsation of freedom in every line of it; a noble rebuke to the foul iniquity about you. . . . It is a great thing in one's life to stand so long and unflinching in the range of the enemy's artillery." On May 28, 1856, Longfellow wrote to Sumner, "I have just been reading again your speech. It is the greatest voice, on the greatest subject, that has been uttered since we became a nation. . . . You have torn the mask off the faces of traitors; and at last the spirit of the North is aroused."
p. 93: And in his account . . . societies: *Longfellow House*, "Research," p. 7. Here's a small sample from Longfellow's account books about his donations. (Note that two dollars in 1856 is equal

to roughly sixty dollars today.) "1853: Nov. 24, Mr. Still (slave), $5.00; Dec. 10, Miss Wormeley for Slave, $10.00. 1854: Jan. 25, For Slaves, $3.00; Feb. 16, Slaves in Canada, $5.00; March 29, Negro Church Buffalo, $2.00; June 29, Mr. Spence Negro School, $3.00. 1855: March 30, For a Fugitive Slave, $5.00; April 29, Mr. Spense Afr. School, $5.00. 1856: May 20, Michigan Negro School, $15.00; Dec., Loyd, the "Nubian Prince," $20.00." (Leo Loyd [also Lloyd in some accounts] was an escaped enslaved man who lectured in the Brooklyn, NY, church of Reverend Samuel Longfellow, Henry's brother.) (H. Longfellow, *Account Books*, pp. 179–81.)

p. 93: "placid stream . . . river": E. Longfellow, p. 29. Ernest wrote that his father "always thought it best not to do a thing. He had none of the adventurous spirit. 'To stay at home is best,' he wrote. He hated excess or extremes. . . . He was not a rushing river, boiling and tumbling over the rocks, but the placid stream flowing through the quiet meadows" (ibid., pp. 28–29).

p. 93: "a crime . . . recoils": C. Sumner, *Crime*, p. 15.

p. 93: That's when a . . . fields: Wallenstein, p. 23.

p. 93, sidebar: His painting . . . shown working and "a man of independent . . . craft": H. Williams, p. 24.

p. 94: "iniquitous," "nefarious," "not agree . . . trade," and Abraham Baldwin . . . individual states: Bowen, pp. 201–03.

p. 94: Point one: when adding up . . . must end in 1808: ibid., pp. 313, 317, and 321.

p. 94: Meanwhile . . . in 1848: "Chronology—Who Banned Slavery When?" Reuters, March 22, 2007, www.reuters.com/article/uk-slavery-idUSL1561464920070322.

p. 94, sidebar: On October 13 . . . Ride": H. Longfellow, "Paul Revere's Ride," n.p.

p. 94, sidebar: "fine piece . . . painting" and "It seems to me . . . say?": Austin, p. 86.

p. 95: "I long . . . poem from you": Hilen, vol. 4, p. 66.

p. 95: "I groan . . . uttering it": ibid., p. 65.

p. 95: Like all great . . . poetically: Irmscher, p. 84. Emily Dickinson was another great American poet who lived at the same time (and in the same state) as Longfellow. Her advice to anyone writing of vexing issues was "tell all the truth, but tell it slant" (Franklin, p. 494). In other words, sometimes the truth is so painful or so overwhelming that it can't be faced head on. Instead, the poet's truth must "dazzle gradually" (ibid.). In an essay about Emily Dickinson, twentieth-century poet Adrienne Rich says, "It is always what is under pressure in us, especially under pressure of concealment—that explodes into poetry" (Gilbert, p. 102). That could be said about Longfellow and "Paul Revere's Ride" as well.

p. 95, sidebar: On December 18 . . . (hemorrhoids): *Boston Evening Transcript*, December 18, 1860, p. 1.

p. 95, sidebar: Longfellow had accidentally . . . for Fields: Austin, p. 86.

p. 96: "to shape the way . . . their past" and it's safe . . . slavery: Gioia, pp. 1–2.

p. 96: "reverberated . . . drum roll" and "one man . . . noble cause": Fischer, p. 331.

p. 96: "invoking . . . cause": Sorby, p. 16.

p. 96: "it cannot . . . our Civil War": Underwood, p. 207.

p. 96: "written to have . . . impending war": Kennedy, p. 298.

p. 96: A 1913 . . . wake-up call: McMurry, p. 188.

p. 96: "Minute Men of '61": Nason, title page.

p. 97: Among those . . . Paul Revere's grandsons: Fischer, p. 298.

p. 97: In Acton . . . to fight: Fletcher, p. 285.

p. 97: "several men . . . volunteered" and "the families. . . service": Hudson, p. 305.

p. 97: "forth to fight . . . '75": "VIII. Civil War," Concord Free Public Library Broadside Collection, n.d., accessed July 18, 2018, www.concordlibrary.org/special-collections/antislavery/08_essay.

p. 97: "well over three million": Foner, p. 1.
p. 97, sidebar: Two of Paul Revere's grandsons . . . until 1880: Fischer, p. 298.
p. 97, sidebar: He spent a . . . young Longfellow: Calhoun, p. 226.
p. 97, sidebar: Charley returned . . . nicked his spine: ibid., p. 228.
p. 98: "an imposing sight . . . for freedom": S. Longfellow, *Life*, vol. 2, p. 393.
p. 99: "The stupendous . . . breath away": Hilen, vol. 4, p. 484.
p. 99: "Neither slavery . . . United States": Lincoln, p. 60. Those *not* granted freedom under the Emancipation Proclamation included "the 450,000 enslaved people in Delaware, Kentucky, Maryland, and Missouri," which were border states that did not secede from the Union. Also denied their freedom "were the 275,000 in Union-occupied Tennessee, and tens of thousands more in portions of Louisiana and Virginia under the control of federal armies" (Foner, p. 1).
p. 99: Across the South . . . American history: Foner, pp. 353–55.
p. 99: "political revolution": ibid., p. 355.
p. 99: The governor . . . undermine civilization: ibid., p. 330.
p. 99: "In some parts . . . on election day": ibid., p. 343.
p. 99: In 1866 . . . "a nameless terror among negroes": ibid., p. 342.
p. 99: Many states . . . poverty: ibid., p. 199.
p. 100: Hoping to reverse . . . short time: ibid., p. 457.
p. 100: By the time . . . just twelve years after it began: ibid., pp. 580–82. A Black man from Louisiana lamented that, "The whole South—every state in the South had got into the hands of the very men that held us as slaves" (ibid., p. 582).
p. 100: "a house divided": In June 1858, at a Republican Party convention in Springfield, Illinois, Abraham Lincoln referred to the United States as a "house divided." Such a house, he said, "divided against itself cannot stand" (Carl Sandburg, *Abraham Lincoln: The Prairie Years and The War Years*, One Volume Edition. [San Diego, CA: Harcourt, Inc., 1954], pp. 137–38).
p. 100: In 1878 . . . Tennessee and "It was like . . . all over again": Hilen, vol. 6, p. 388.
p. 100: Longfellow continued . . . month of his life: Irmscher, p. 115.
p. 100: "the true mission . . . their ragged opinions": Wagenknecht, p. 56.
p. 101: Longfellow's three . . . hillside: S. Longfellow, *Final Memorials*, vol. 1, p. 237. Longfellow might have attended were he not in pain. In his journal for April 18, 1875, he wrote, "Bad day for me; neuralgia raging. In the evening, my girls drive over to Prospect Hill to see the lighting of Paul Revere's signal lanterns in the belfry of the old North Church." The three Longfellow girls also attended the celebration in Concord the following day. Longfellow wrote, "I could not go, but was glad they should have this historic memory" (ibid.).
p. 101: Revere sitting . . . in Boston: *Paul Revere Heritage Project*, n.p.
p. 101: "grand crescendo . . . fortissimo": Fischer, p. 334.
p. 103: "One of my earliest . . . Ride'": *Longfellow House*, "Remembers," p. 1. Senator Kennedy said that his mother, Rose, felt that "Longfellow's poem was a wonderful way for her children to learn about poetry and history at the same time. That early exposure to our nation's history and literature had . . . an immeasurable impact on my life."
p. 103: We know . . . write a letter and "first senatorial . . . slam": ibid, p. 5.

Bibliography

While researching and writing this book, I consulted sources from the eighteenth, nineteenth, twentieth, and twenty-first centuries. I visited libraries and historical societies in Concord, Lexington, Cambridge, Boston, New York, and London. I talked to and emailed a number of professors and historians. This is a selected bibliography, created from my full list.

Adams, Hannah. *A Summary History of New-England*. Dedham, MA: H. Mann and J. H. Adams, 1799.

Adams, Josiah. *An Address Delivered at Acton, July 21, 1835, Being the First Centennial Anniversary of the Organization of That Town*. Boston: J. T. Buckingham, 1835.

Alden, John Richard. *General Gage in America*. Baton Rouge: Louisiana State University Press, 1948.

Allan, Herbert S. *John Hancock: Patriot in Purple*. New York: Beechhurst Press, 1953.

Archer, Richard. *As If an Enemy's Country*. New York: Oxford University Press, 2010.

Atlantic Monthly, "Atlantic Advertiser and Miscellany," vol. 22. August 1868, p. 256.

Austin, James C. *Fields of the Atlantic Monthly*. San Marino, CA: Henry E. Huntington Library, 1953.

Bacheller, Carrie E. *Munroe Tavern: The Custodian's Story*. Lexington, MA: Lexington Historical Society, 1924.

Bahne, Charles. "One Hundred and Fifty Years of 'Paul Revere's Ride'—A Sesquicentennial Observation." *Revere House Gazette*, Summer 2010, no. 99, p. 3.

Baldwin, Alice. *The New England Clergy and the American Revolution*. Durham, NC: Duke University Press, 1927.

Bancroft, George. *History of the Colonization of the United States*. 2 vols. Boston: Charles Bowen, 1837.

Bardeen, Charles William. *Authors' Birthdays*. Syracuse, NY: C. W. Bardeen, 1898.

Barker, John. *The British in Boston*. Cambridge, MA: Harvard University Press, 1926.

Barrett, Mary Prescott. "Events at Col. Barrett's Farm and Concord, April 19, 1775: Mrs. Peter Barrett [Mary Prescott] Interview with Lemuel Shattuck, 1831." www.nps.gov/mima/learn/historyculture/upload/Barrett-Farm-HSR-Appendix-Creduced.pdf.

Barrett, Nathan III. "Reminiscences." Allen French–Ruth Wheeler Collection. Special Collections, Concord Free Public Library, Concord, MA.

Bartlett, Joseph. *Gregory Stone Genealogy*. Boston: Stone Family Association, 1918.

Basler, Roy P., ed. *The Collected Works of Abraham Lincoln*. 8 vols. New Brunswick, NJ: Rutgers University Press, 1953.

Belknap, Dr. Jeremy. "Journal of My Tour to the Camp and Observations I Made There." *Proceedings of the Massachusetts Historical Society, No. 4, 1858–1860*. Boston: Massachusetts Historical Society, 1860, pp. 77–86.

Benton, J. H. *Early Census Making in Massachusetts*. Boston: Charles E. Goodspeed, 1905.

Bowen, Catherine Drinker. *Miracle at Philadelphia*. Boston: Little, Brown, 1966.

Broadside. April 17, 1861. Special Collections, Concord Free Public Library, Concord, MA. www.concordlibrary.org/special-collections/buildinghistories/townhouse/civilWar.

Brooks, Van Wyck. *The Flowering of New England 1815–1865*. New York: Modern Library, 1937.

Brown, Abram English. *Beneath Old Roof Trees*. Boston: Lee and Shepard, 1896.

Brown, Rebecca Warren. *Stories About General Warren*. Boston: James Loring, 1835.

Buckingham, J. T. "Early American Artists and Mechanics, No. II, Paul Revere." *New-England Magazine*, vol. 3. Boston: J. T. and E. Buckingham, 1832, pp. 305–314.

Calhoun, Charles C. *Longfellow, A Rediscovered Life*. Boston: Beacon Press, 2004.

Carter, Clarence Edwin. *The Correspondence of General Thomas Gage*. 2 vols. Hamden, CT: Archon Books, 1969. First published in 1931 by Yale University Press.

Castle, Norman, ed. *The Minute Men, 1775–1975*. Southborough, MA: Yankee Color Corporation, 1977.

Chan, Alexandra. *Slavery in the Age of Reason*. Knoxville: University of Tennessee Press, 2007.

Chase, Ellen. *The Beginnings of the American Revolution*. 3 vols. New York: Baker and Taylor, 1910.

Clarke, Betty. "Extracts from Letter of Miss Betty Clarke, Daughter of Rev. Jonas Clarke." *Proceedings of the Lexington Historical Society*. Lexington, MA: Lexington Historical Society, 1912.

Clarke, Jonas. *The Battle of Lexington: A Sermon and Eyewitness Narrative*. Ventura, CA: Nordskog Publishing, 2007.

———. *Diary*. Manuscript, Vol. 2. Lexington, MA: Lexington Historical Society, 1775.

Coburn, Frank Warren. *The Battle of April 19, 1775: In Lexington, Concord, Lincoln, Arlington, Cambridge, Somerville, and Charlestown, Massachusetts*. Lexington, MA: Frank Coburn, 1912.

Crawford, Mary Caroline. *Old Boston Days and Ways*. Boston: Little, Brown, 1909.

Curtis, George William. *Proceedings at the Centennial Celebration of the Concord Fight, April 19, 1875*. Concord, MA: Town of Concord, 1876.

Curtis, Wayne. *And a Bottle of Rum: A History of the World in Ten Cocktails*. New York: Three Rivers Press, 2006.

Cutter, William R. *Genealogical and Personal Memoirs Relating to the Families of Boston and Eastern Massachusetts*. New York: Lewis Historical, 1908.

Detail and Conduct of the American War, 3rd ed. London: Richardson and Urquhart, 1780.

Drake, Samuel Adams. *History of Middlesex County, Massachusetts*. 2 vols. Boston: Estes and Lauriat, 1880.

Dray, Philip. *There Is Power in a Union*. New York: Anchor Books, 2011.

Eaton, Wyatt. "Recollections of American Poets," *Century Illustrated Monthly Magazine*, vol. 64, May–October 1902.

Emerson, Amelia, ed. *Diary and Letters of William Emerson, 1743–1776*. Madison: University of Wisconsin Press, 1972.

Fields, Annie. *Authors and Friends*. Boston: Houghton Mifflin, 1897.

Fischer, David Hackett. *Paul Revere's Ride*. New York: Oxford Press, 1994.

Fletcher, James. *Acton in History*. Philadelphia: J. W. Lewis, 1890.

Flexner, James Thomas. *George Washington in the American Revolution (1775–1783)*. Boston: Little, Brown, 1967.

Foner, Eric. *Reconstruction: America's Unfinished Revolution*. New York: Harper and Row, 1988.

Force, Peter, ed. *American Archives*, series 4, vol. 2. Washington, DC: Prepared and Published Under Authority of an Act of Congress, 1837–1853.

Forman, Samuel A. *Dr. Joseph Warren: The Boston Tea Party, Bunker Hill, and the Birth of American Liberty*. Gretna, LA: Pelican Publishing, 2012.

Franklin, R. W. *The Poems of Emily Dickinson*. Cambridge, MA: Belknap Press of Harvard University Press, 1999.

French, Allen. *The Day of Concord and Lexington*. Boston: Little, Brown, 1925.

———. *General Gage's Informers*. New York: Greenwood Press, 1968.

Frothingham, Richard. *History of the Siege of Boston and of the Battles of Lexington, Concord, and Bunker Hill*. Boston: Little, Brown, 1851.

———. *Life and Times of Joseph Warren*. Boston: Little, Brown, 1865.

Fuhrer, Mary. *Research for the Re-Interpretation of the Buckman Tavern*. Lexington, MA: Lexington Historical Society, 2012.

Gale, Robert. *A Henry Wadsworth Longfellow Companion*. Westport, CT: Greenwood Press, 2003.

Galvin, John R. *The Minute Men: The First Fight: Myths and Realities of the Revolutionary War*. Washington, DC: Potomac Books, 1989.

Gilbert, Sandra, and Susan Gubar, eds. *Shakespeare's Sisters: Feminist Essays on Women Poets*. Bloomington: Indiana University Press, 1979.

Gordon, William. "An Account of the Commencement of Hostilities Between Great Britain and America." May 17, 1775, *American Archives* Series 4, vol. 2, pp. 625–31.

———. *The History of the Rise, Progress, and Establishment of the Independence of the United States of America*. 4 vols. London: Charles Dilly, 1788.

Gioia, Dana. "Henry Wadsworth Longfellow on 'Paul Revere's Ride.'" www.danagioia.com/essays/reviews-and-authors-notes/henry-wadsworth-longfellow-on-paul-reveres-ride.

Gladwell, Malcolm. *The Tipping Point: How Little Things Can Make a Big Difference*. Boston: Little, Brown, 2000.

Goss, Elbridge Henry. *The Life of Colonel Paul Revere*. 2 vols. Boston: Joseph George Cupples, 1891.

Graf, LeRoy P., and Ralph W. Haskins. *The Papers of Andrew Johnson*. 16 vols. Knoxville: University of Tennessee Press, 1967–2000.

Gross, Robert. *The Minutemen and Their World*. New York: Hill and Wang, 1976.

Harrington, Levi. "Account." Transcribed by J. F. Denis in *Compilation of First Hand Accounts*. Lexington, MA: Lexington Historical Society, 1846, pp. 261–67.

Hilen, Andrew. *The Letters of Henry Wadsworth Longfellow*. 6 vols. Cambridge, MA: Belknap Press of Harvard University Press, 1966–1982.

Holland, Henry. *William Dawes and His Ride with Paul Revere*. Boston: John Wilson and Son, 1878.

Hosmer, Josephine. "Memoir of Joseph Hosmer." Concord, MA: Special Collections, Concord Free Public Library, 1869.

Hudson, Charles. *History of the Town of Lexington, Middlesex County, Massachusetts: Genealogies*. 2 vols. Boston: Wiggin and Lunt, 1868.

Hunter, Martin. *Extracts from the Journal of General Sir Martin Hunter*. Edinburgh, Scotland: Edinburgh Press, 1894.

Hurd, Duane Hamilton. *History of Middlesex County, Massachusetts*. 3 vols. Philadelphia: J. W. Lewis, 1890.

Hutchinson, Thomas. *The Diary and Letters of His Excellency Thomas Hutchinson*. 2 vols. London: Sampson Low, Marston, Searle & Rivington, 1883.

Irmscher, Christoph. *Public Poet, Private Man: Henry Wadsworth Longfellow at 200*. Amherst: University of Massachusetts Press, 2009.

Johnson, Carl. *Professor Longfellow of Harvard*. Eugene: University of Oregon Press, 1944.

Keightley, Thomas. *The History of England*. 2 vols. Boston: Hilliard, Gray, 1840.

Kennedy, W. Sloane. *Henry W. Longfellow: Biography, Anecdote, Letters, Criticism*. Akron, OH: Saalfield, 1903.

Kollen, Richard. *Lexington, Massachusetts: From Liberty's Birthplace to Progressive Suburb*. Charleston, SC: History Press, 2004.

———. *Lexington, Massachusetts: Treasures from Historic Archives*. Charleston, SC: History Press, 2006.

———. *The Patriot Parson of Lexington, Massachusetts: Reverend Jonas Clarke and the American Revolution*. Charleston, SC: History Press, 2016.

———. *Letters from the Historian*. www.lexingtonhistory.org/uploads/6/5/2/1/6521332/childreninthehchouse.pdf.

Longfellow House Bulletin, "Discovering the Furry and Feathered Members of the Longfellow Family," June 2009.

———. "Recent Research at the House," June 2012.

———. "Longfellow House Remembers Senator Edward Kennedy," December 2009.

Langguth, A. J. *Patriots: The Men Who Started the American Revolution*. New York: Simon and Schuster, 1988.

Leehey, Patrick, et al. *Paul Revere—Artisan, Businessman and Patriot*. Boston: Paul Revere Memorial Association, 1988.

Lincoln, Abraham. "Emancipation Proclamation." United States National Archives, www.archives.gov/exhibits/featured-documents/emancipation-proclamation.

Lister, Ensign Jeremy. *Concord Fight: Being so much of the Narrative of Ensign Jeremy Lister of the 10th Regiment of Foot as pertains to his services on the 19th of April, 1775, and to his experiences in Boston during the early months of the Siege*. Cambridge, MA: Harvard University Press, 1931.

Longfellow, Alice. "Reminiscences of My Father." Cambridge, MA: Longfellow House, 1895.

———. "Longfellow and His Children." *Youth's Companion, New England Edition*, September 2, 1897.

Longfellow, Ernest Wadsworth. *Random Memories*. Boston: Houghton Mifflin, 1922.

Longfellow, Henry Wadsworth. *Account Books*. Houghton Library, Harvard University, Cambridge, MA. https://iiif.lib.harvard.edu/manifests/view/drs:9028239$11i.

———. "Paul Revere's Ride." *Boston Evening Transcript*, December 18, 1860.

———. "Paul Revere's Ride." Manuscript. MS Am 1340 (105), Houghton Library, Harvard University, Cambridge, MA.

———. *Poems on Slavery*. Cambridge, MA: John Owen, 1842.

Longfellow, Samuel, ed. *Final Memorials of Henry Wadsworth Longfellow*. 2 vols. Boston: Ticknor and Fields, 1887.

———. *Life of Henry Wadsworth Longfellow, with Extracts from His Journals and Correspondence*. 2 vols. Boston: Ticknor, 1886.

Lossing, Benson, J. *Reflections of Rebellion: Hours with the Living Men and Women of the Revolution*. New York: Funk and Wagnalls, 1889. Reprint, Charleston, SC: History Press, 2005. Page references are to the 2005 edition.

Luzader, John F. "Major John Buttrick House." *Minuteman National Historic Park, Historic Structures Report, Part 1, Historical Date Section*. Boston: United States Department of the Interior, 1968, p. 2.

Mackenzie, Frederick. *A British Fusilier in Revolutionary Boston, Being the Diary of Lieutenant Frederick Mackenzie, Adjutant of the Royal Welch Fusiliers, January 5–April 30, 1775*. Cambridge, MA: Harvard University Press, 1926.

MacLean, John. *A Rich Harvest: The History, Buildings, and People of Lincoln, Massachusetts*. Lincoln, MA: Lincoln Historical Society, 1987.

Malcolm, Joyce Lee. "The Scene of the Battle, 1775." *Minuteman National Historic Park, Historic Grounds Report, Cultural Resources Management Study No. 15*. Boston: United States Department of the Interior, 1985, pp. 30–41.

Manegold, C. S. *Ten Hills Farm: The Forgotten History of Slavery in the North*. Princeton, NJ: Princeton University Press, 2010.

Marshall, Traute M. *Art Museums Plus: Cultural Excursions in New England*. Lebanon, NH: University of New England Press, 2009.

McKenzie, Alexander. "Washington in Cambridge," *Atlantic Monthly*, July 1875, pp. 92–98.

McMurry, Charles Alexander. *Public School Methods*, vol. 3. Chicago: Hanson Bellows, 1913.

Miller, John C. *Sam Adams: Pioneer in Propaganda*. Stanford, CA: Stanford University Press, 1936.

Morrison, Samuel Eliot. *Oxford History of the American People*. New York: Oxford University Press, 1965.

Murdock, Harold. *The Nineteenth of April 1775*. Boston: Houghton Mifflin, 1925.

Nason, George W. *History and Complete Roster of the Massachusetts Regiments: Minute Men of '61*. Boston: Smith and McCance, 1910.

O'Brien, Harriet, ed. *Paul Revere's Own Story.* Boston: Perry Walton, 1929.

Olson, Donald. *Celestial Sleuth.* New York: Springer Publishing, 2013.

Parker, Charles Symmes. *Town of Arlington, Past and Present.* Arlington, MA: C. S. Parker and Son, 1907.

Paul Revere Heritage Project. Boston University Graduate History Club. www.paul-revere-heritage.com.

Paul Revere Memorial Association. *Paul Revere in Primary Sources: Ten Documents with Transcriptions and Glossaries, a Time Line of Revere's Life, and Revere Family Genealogy.* Boston: Paul Revere Memorial Association, 2005.

Pearl, Sydelle. *Dear Mr. Longfellow: Letters to and from the Children's Poet.* Amherst, NY: Prometheus Books, 2012.

Perry, Williams Stevens. *Historical Collections Relating to American Colonial Churches.* 5 vols. Hartford, CT: Church Press, 1871–1878.

Phinney, Elias. *History of the Battle of Lexington.* Boston: Phelps and Farnham, 1825.

Powers, Ella M. "A History Lesson." *Primary Education,* January 1912, p. 224–25.

Prescott, Olive Ann. *Colonel John Robinson.* Forge Village, MA: Murray Printing Company, 1967. First printed by Lowell Mail Print, 1896.

Pruitt, Bettye, ed. *The Massachusetts Tax Valuation List of 1771.* Boston: G. K. Hall, 1978. http://sites.fas.harvard.edu/~hsb41/masstax/masstax.cgi.

Rantoul, Robert, Jr. *An Oration Delivered at Concord: On the Celebration of the Seventy-fifth Anniversary of the Events of April 19, 1775.* Boston: Dutton and Wentworth, 1850.

Revere, Paul. *Paul Revere's Three Accounts of His Famous Ride,* "The Deposition: Draft," "The Deposition: Corrected Copy," and "To Jeremy Belknap." Boston: Massachusetts Historical Society, 2000.

Revolutionary-Era Concord Town Records, 1775, January 2–December 29. Special Collections, Concord Free Public Library, Concord, MA.

Ripley, Ezra. *A History of the Fight at Concord.* Concord, MA: Herman Atwill, 1832.

Rowe, John. *The Diary of John Rowe, 1764–1779.* Cambridge, MA: John Wilson and Son, 1895.

Ryan, Michael. *Concord and the Dawn of Revolution.* Charleston, SC: History Press, 2007.

Sabin, Douglas. *April 19, 1775: A Historiographical Study.* Cascade, ID: Sinclair Street, 2011.

Schott, Thomas E. *Alexander H. Stephens of Georgia: A Biography.* Baton Rouge: Louisiana State University Press, 1996.

Schultz, Eric, and Michael Tougias. *King Philip's War.* Woodstock, VT: Countryman Press, 1999.

Sears, Lorenzo. *John Hancock: The Picturesque Patriot.* Boston: Little, Brown, 1913.

Shattuck, Lemuel. *History of the Town of Concord.* Boston: Russell, Odiorne, 1835.

Sheets, Robert Newman. *Robert Newman: The Life and Times of the Sexton.* Denver: Newman Family Society, 1975.

Smith, Paul. "The American Loyalists: Notes on Their Organization and Numerical Strength." *The William and Mary Quarterly,* vol. 25, no. 2 (April 1968), pp. 259–77.

Smith, Samuel Abbot. *West Cambridge 1775.* Somerville, MA: Fleming and Son, 1974. First published Boston: Alfred Mudge and Son, 1864. Page references are to the 1974 edition.

Sorby, Angela. *Schoolroom Poets.* Durham: University of New Hampshire Press, 2005.

Standage, Tom. *A History of the World in Six Glasses.* New York: Walker, 2005.

Stearns, Frank Preston. *Cambridge Sketches.* Philadelphia: J. B. Lippincott, 1905.

Sumner, Charles. *The Crime Against Kansas.* Boston: John P. Jewett, 1856.

———. *The Works of Charles Sumner.* 20 vols. Boston: Lee and Shepard, 1870–1900.

Sumner, General William H. "Reminiscences by General William H. Sumner." *New England Historical and Genealogical Register,* no. 8, 1854, pp. 187–91.

Sutherland, Lieutenant William. *Narrative. Late News of the Excursions and Ravages of the King's Troops On the nineteenth of April, 1775.* Cambridge, MA: Harvard College Press, 1927, pp. 13–24.

Tax Records, Concord East Book, 1774. Special Collections, Concord Free Public Library, Concord, MA.

Tourtellot, Arthur. *Lexington and Concord: The Beginning of the War of the American Revolution*. New York: W. W. Norton, 1959.

Triber, Jayne E. *A True Republican: The Life of Paul Revere*. Amherst: University of Massachusetts Press, 1998.

True, Henry. *Journal and Letters of Rev. Henry True*. Marion, OH: Star Press, 1900.

Tucker-Macchetta, Blanche Roosevelt. *The Home Life of Henry W. Longfellow*. New York: G. W. Carleton, 1882.

Tyler, J. E., "An Account of Lexington in the Rockingham Mss. at Sheffield," *The William and Mary Quarterly*, vol. 10, no. 1 (January 1953), pp. 99–107.

Underwood, Francis H. *Henry Wadsworth Longfellow: A Biographical Sketch*. London: George Routledge and Sons, 1882.

Unger, Harlow G. *John Hancock: Merchant King and American Patriot*. New York: John Wiley and Sons, 2000.

Varney, George. *The Story of Patriots' Day, Lexington and Concord, April 19, 1775*. Boston: Lee and Shepard, 1895.

Wagenknecht, Edward. *Henry Wadsworth Longfellow: Portrait of an American Humanist*. New York: Oxford Press, 1966.

Wallenstein, Peter. *Cradle of America*. Lawrence: University Press of Kansas, 2007.

Warren-Adams Letters, Being Chiefly a Correspondence Among John Adams, Samuel Adams and James Warren. 2 vols. Boston: Massachusetts Historical Society, 1917 and 1925.

Warren, Mercy Otis. *History of the Rise, Progress and Termination of the American Revolution*. 3 vols. Boston: E. Larkin, 1805.

Wellman, Thomas. *History of the Town of Lynnfield*. Boston: Blanchard Watts Engraving Company, 1895.

Wells, William V. *The Life and Public Services of Samuel Adams*. 2 vols. Boston: Little, Brown, 1865.

Wheildon, William. *New Chapter in the History of the Concord Fight*. Boston: Lee and Shepard, 1885.

———. *History of Paul Revere's Signal Lanterns*. Boston: Lee and Shepard, 1878.

Willard, Margaret Wheeler, ed. *Letters on the American Revolution, 1774–1776*. Boston: Houghton Mifflin, 1925.

Williams, Basil. *The Whig Supremacy*. Oxford, England: Oxford University Press, 1939.

Williams, Hermann Warner Jr. *Mirror to the American Past, 1750–1900*. Greenwich, CT: New York Graphic Society, 1973.

Winsor, Justin. *The Memorial History of Boston*. 4 vols. Boston: James R. Osgood, 1882.

Wood, Gordon. *The Radicalism of the American Revolution*. New York: Vintage Books, 1991.

Woodbury, Ellen Carolina De Quincy. *Dorothy Quincy, Wife of John Hancock*. Washington, DC: Neale Publishing Company, 1905.

Zellner, Carl. "The Opposite Shore: Charlestown's Role in Paul Revere's Ride." *Revere House Gazette*, Summer 1999.

———. "Paul Revere's Rowers." *Revere House Gazette*, Spring 2000.

———. "Revere's Rowers." Unpublished preliminary draft, January 25, 1999. Provided to the author in email correspondence.

———. "Where Was Paul Revere's Landing?" Unpublished manuscript, October 4, 1997. Provided to the author in email correspondence.

Zilversmit, Arthur. "Quok Walker, Mumbet, and the Abolition of Slavery in Massachusetts," *The William and Mary Quarterly*, vol. 25, no. 4 (October 1968), pp. 614–24.

Image Credits

Front cover
Karen Boss

Title page
Karen Boss

Chapter openers
Library of Congress, Geography and Map Division (LCCN: gm71002357)

The Poem
Library of Congress, Prints and Photographs Division (LCCN: 2018645334): page viii
From *Paul Revere: The Torch Bearer of the Revolution*, Belle Moses, 1916: page xiii

Prologue
Wikimedia Commons photograph of *Portrait of Paul Revere*: page xvi
Karen Boss: page xxii
Library of Congress, Prints and Photographs Division (LCCN: 2015650276): page xxiv

Chapter 1
Library of Congress, Prints and Photographs Division (LCCN: 2004666667): page xxvi
Library of Congress, Prints and Photographs Division (LCCN: 2001699854): page 3
Library of Congress, Geography and Map Division (LCCN: 2018590028): pages 4 & 5
Wikimedia Commons photograph of *Portrait of Margaret Kemble Gage*: page 7
Library of Congress, Prints and Photographs Division (LCCN: 2004672092): page 10
Library of Congress, Prints and Photographs Division (LCCN: 2001696978): page 11

Chapter 2
Karen Boss: page 12
Wikimedia Commons photograph of lantern: page 15
Library of Congress, Geography and Map Division (LCCN: gm71000620): page 16

Chapter 3
Historic New England, from New England Mutual Life Insurance Company 1888 calendar: page 18
Library of Congress, Geography and Map Division (LCCN: gm71000916): page 22
Boston Public Library, Boston Pictorial Archive: page 24

Chapter 4
Karen Boss: page 26
Boston Public Library, Archive of Photographic Documentation of Early Massachusetts Architecture: page 31

Chapter 5
Bromley & Company, Inc. postcard of *Midnight Ride of Paul Revere*: page 32
Boston Public Library, The Tichnor Brothers Collection: page 34
Jeff Lantos: page 40 & 41

Chapter 6
National Archives (item 208-FS-3200-5): page 42
Diane M. Earley: page 44

Chapter 7
Diane M. Earley: page 48
Wikimedia Commons photograph of a William Dawes portrait: page 51
Diane M. Earley: page 54

Chapter 8
Diane M. Earley: page 56
Library of Congress, Prints and Photographs Division (LCCN: 2016794230): page 65

Chapter 9
Library of Congress, Prints and Photographs Division (loc.gov/pictures/resource/pga.14059): page 66
Plastichrome by Colourpicture postcard of *The Dawn of Liberty*: page 69
Diane M. Earley: page 71

Chapter 10
Diane M. Earley: page 72
Wikimedia Commons photograph of *Plate II: A View of the Town of Concord*: page 76
Courtesy of the Boston Public Library, Leslie Jones Collection: page 80

Chapter 11
From *A Brief History of the United States* by Joel Dorman Steele and Esther Baker Steele, 1885: page 84

Chapter 12
Library of Congress, Prints and Photographs Division (LCCN: 2004665361): page 90
Library of Congress, Prints and Photographs Division (Reproduction number: LC-DIG-pga-01949): page 98
E. T. Paull Music Company, scan of sheet music for "Paul Revere's Ride March-TwoStep": page 101
Karen Boss: page 102

Index

Page numbers in *italics* indicate illustrations.